using

THE UGLY DU

to find

The Missing Link

between boys and men

Nick Clements

Sound of the heart publishing

using

THE UGLY DUCKLING

to find

The Missing Link

between boys and men

Nick Clements

Published in 2008 by
Sound of the heart
PO Box 557
Swansea SA8 4WJ

www.soundoftheheart.com

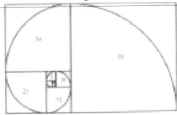

ISBN 0-9547302-2-4
Writing, cover photography, and all illustrations © Nick Clements 2007
Thank you to Mohinder, Kate, Julian, Bear, Mark and Sophie for spending the time to
read and help me with this book.

Dedicated to my two beautiful children, Tom and Anna.
To all the men who hold and care for the bundle.
To the Samburu people and all the other tribes to which I belong,
knowingly, and unknowingly.
To Sophie, Manda, and all the people who have supported and
encouraged me on my journey.

To my mum

CONTENTS

PREFACE

★   *My name is Nicholas Peter Clements. I was born in London in 1956. I have two grown up children, Tom and Anna.*
★   *My father was called Richard, my mother Bridget, I have a brother called Robert.*
★   *I was a boy, a teenager, a man, I am a father, and I have been initiated into eldership within a tribe in Africa.*
★   *I was brought up in Britain, spend most of my life working in Wales, and am now employed throughout the world.*

In 2003 I brought the Pioneers Art Group to an end after 22 years of successful trading. In 2004 I went on a vision quest on Dartmoor, asking the question *"do I want to stay together with my wife"* and I returned with a tough answer. We separated after 26 years together. In 2006 I was invited to Kenya to document the ritual circumcision of boys by the Samburu tribe. My father died. My children left home, one married, the other went to College. Throughout these turbulent years I worked on ideas about rites of passage, using the story *"The Ugly Duckling"*. I am very grateful to Eric Haugaard, whose recent translation I quote. This is the fruit of all those labours.

We live in turbulent and changing times, there are many difficult decisions being made, or being ignored, all over the world. The issues of environmental change, globalization, materialism, war and fundamentalism, surround and bombard us. We can react fearfully to these issues, we can choose to ignore them, we can blame others for them, or we can stand up and face them. This book deals with one of those issues – the trouble with teenage boys. Such an issue can't be dealt with in isolation, in order to create sustainable solutions, I will have to stray into other territories, but I will always be returning to this issue.

By the very nature of this work I owe a lot to Robert Bly, his book *"Iron John"*, and the men's movement. I acknowledge my indebtedness and respect for his work, his beautiful words, and his insights into the human condition. It is almost 20 years since his book was first published, and I feel it needs to be made more accessible. I know a great many people who have heard of him, and of the book, but few have ever read it. I am using a more immediate story, one we all know, in order that more people can look at these issues and enter the debate. *"The Ugly Duckling"* has been bastardized by many people - Victorian scholars, Walt Disney, and many more. The translation I use is direct from the Danish and reproduces Hans Christian Andersen's intended style. It is time to reclaim the story as an outstanding, dark, and moving tale, written as an autobiographical treatise by an accomplished storyteller, who had found his soul's purpose. It is a metaphor for a boy growing up without a father. It documents the trials and tribulations of such an ascent into adulthood, and details the many ways in which he is tested and challenged. We have an ever-increasing number of these people in our midst. I will use the story to illustrate the pitfalls of such a lonely existence, and to emphasize the need for supervised rites of passage at this time in boys' lives. I witnessed and participated in such a ritual on the desolate plains of northern Kenya, and spent time with a semi-nomadic tribe trying to understand what it was and why they were so committed to such a ritual. I use examples from this experience and others to re-iterate my commitment to rites, and to note the importance of elders, older men, in these events. In order to make these points I will have to address the wider issue of parenting, and the significance of our connection with the natural world. The value of rites of passage applies not just to teenage boys, but to all of us. Women and men can gain insights into life from this practice. I am arguing for rites of passage, but I am not telling you how to do them. I think the creation of a definitive guide to teenage boy rites of passage would be dangerous and divisive. This book is a positive polemic for community-led rites of passage, and everything that entails.

Rites of passage, these three words can lead to a great deal of confusion and debate, in terms of what they actually mean. So, before we go any further, here is where I am coming from. My present understanding is condensed into the belief that I will go through 'ages' or stages. Put simply, these are being a baby, becoming a child, becoming a father, etc. Rites of passage need to occur before each age, but nowadays, we seem to be only aware of the teenage rites of passage. It is best if we are helped by our elders during the change between each age. As we enter the next age, we need guidance, advice and encouragment to take on the next level of responsibility and awareness, indeed, a teenager or a father is not aware of the responsibilities he will have in the next age, he needs mentoring. At present we have lost contact with this view, and we allow all our people to move up through the ages without help or encouragment. We have a 'peer initiation' society, helped through our rites by our peers not our elders. This is not the easiest way and leads to a great many problems, as our peers don't know what is waiting for us in the future - they, like us, haven't been there yet. We continue to age, but there is a great deal of pain, damage and blind thrashing, because of the lack of mentoring by elders. A 'supervised' community supported rite of passage would cut out all this thrashing, it would be precise, sharp and quick. It would be a 'homeopathic' condensed version of the next age to which the individual is coming. It needs to be important to everyone, it would be run by elders, and it would be given time and a great deal of thought. In such rites the individual is tested, and has to pass certain lessons, in order to then receive approval and praise from the whole community for moving on to the next age. By their very nature they include challenge, danger, bonding, fear, reward, and, if you succed in passing them, peace of mind.

INTRODUCTION

I work as a community artists, a ceremonialist, and facilitator of men's work. These are not often used as job titles, some people find it easier to call me a 'catalyst'. The dictionary includes these two definitions:

A person or thing that precipitates an event or change

A person whose talk, enthusiasm, or energy causes others to be more friendly, enthusiastic or energetic

I hope by reading this book I will perform one or more of these functions in your life. I need to stress, however, I am not trying to impart a dogma. My role is merely to reflect on my own and others experiences and to talk about these in an enthusiastic manner. Please do not think I am offering solutions to yours or other people's specific problems.

The wastelands

I am a man who spent the last thirty years working directly with the disenfranchised, vulnerable, and desperate people who inhabit the dark underbelly avoided and ignored by mainstream Western culture. I have worked in some of the most deprived and devastated communities. In the South Wales Valleys during the Thatcherite clearances. The desperate communities of Eastern Germany, following the fall of communism. With the cardboard families of the Bronx in New York, burnt out by their landlords' greed and avarice. Over thirty years on the incomprehensible council estates of big cities. The forgotten wastelands of concrete, broken glass, ignorance, abuse and boarded windows. Working with the effects of neglect - violence, criminality, addiction, depression, mental illness, loss of hope, lack of connection to grief, and the cruelty of being deprived from birth. We witness the disasters in Africa with righteous despair, but there are similar and more invidious ones happening right here in the heartlands of the richest and most conspicuously affluent societies. We are so familiar with these disasters we don't even recognize them as such.

When people believe their lives depend on money, artifacts and material goods you are in trouble. When those people loose their connection to community, love, mutual indebtedness and reciprocity it really is dangerous for the world. We are breeding bullies, dealing in unhappiness, greed and selfishness- indeed we encourage and support such attitudes. Our culture depends on our fear and frustration for its perpetuation. We see the world in a very peculiar and skewed way, not considering the whole or bigger picture. This way of viewing the world is, in my opinion, immature. The immature boy is selfish and spoilt. He stamps his feet when he doesn't receive what he feels he is due. In that sense, we are an uninitiated people – we have for many years chosen to ignoring the obvious, and only focus on our personal needs. With the increased awareness of the interconnected nature of the world, our efforts to assist our African and indigenous brothers and sisters, our environmental and ecological concerns, our recognition of the value of nutrition, we are starting to show some maturity. For me, these are signs of our

1

seeking initiation. Those are the first steps towards our initiation to becoming mature human beings. These are the steps all teenagers need to take.

Teenagers

Teenagers seem to be blamed for a lot of our society's woes at present. Teenagers are not the problem. They are only expressing a discontent we all feel. Teenagers have always asked the question *"why"* and the culture ignoring such a question is in trouble. We expect our teenagers to somehow, innately, grow up without any assistance or commitment from ourselves. They are trying their hardest to do this, to please us, to conform to what we want. We are the ones letting them down, not the other way around. Only when we come to terms with this will we start repairing the damage. You cannot 'treat' the problem that is 'teenagers' without first understanding why they behave like they do. They are seeking to create their own identity, they are trying to become as unique and beautiful beings as possible. This takes time, mistakes, and lots of understanding. We need to encourage them in this, we need to support such activities. We need to incorporate such activities into our society, not outlaw them.

The attitude we have towards teenagers reminds me of our attitude towards litter. For many of us when we are out in the countryside, enjoying nature, there comes a moment when we are confronted by other peoples' litter. In this moment we can react in a variety of ways. We can become angered by the insensitivity of those individuals who leave their litter in such beautiful surroundings. We can wonder what the council or local authority is doing about this problem, but not contact them. In both instances we walk on by, and the litter remains where it is. When I go out on local walks I take a plastic bag with me, *I don't do this every time, I'm not claiming to be a saint!* I collect a bit of rubbish every now and again. If everyone were to complain to the council, something might happen. If everyone were to now and again collect a bit of rubbish, something might happen. There are many approaches to the problem, and they all create a solution. The one reaction not creating a solution is being angry by yourself. We need to translate this into our lives, not only in terms of litter, but also teenagers. Every now and again I go out and work with teenagers, and in those moments I become part of the solution. Some people will spend large amounts of their lives, or make a career from doing this. It is everyone's responsibility in the end, if you have no children, or your children are very young, or old. Don't walk past and expect someone else to sort out the problem. This is vitally important work, especially important, for the future of the planet.

Teenagers need to be forceful in order to free themselves from the gravitational pull of the family. To break away there needs to dynamism, change and strength. At the point of separation they are confused. Thus far they have been defined by family, and now they needs to re-define themselves. This applies to boys and girls, but throughout this book I will focus on the boys. The creation of the individual rather than the son or daughter of the mother is vital work. To do it successfully the individual needs to be exposed to three elements:-

2

✱ *To go within and find himself, see who he really is, not the person his parents and siblings wanted him to be.*

✱ *To find his peers with whom he can compare himself, and with whom he can form friendships and rivalries.*

✱ *To find his elders, his role models, from whom he can learn about the world beyond the family, and through whom he can aspire.*

The dynamic pull between his family, himself, his peers and elders creates the new person, it is the process of individuation. The force propelling us from birth through to eldership is so strong it creates a trajectory called pre-destination. The path we chose before we were born is represented in this story by the swan. He starts life as a swan, and he always is a swan, finally, he sees it for himself. Along the way he looses connection with this simple truth. We are all like him. We start out strongly knowing who we are, and what we need to do in life. However, we are swayed, influenced and often - as with the swan - beaten or forced into a different way of being. We become confused, we accept our labels, we are bullied or we become bullies. We can fool ourselves we are happy like this, we can con ourselves into believing it is true, but there is always a nagging doubt. That doubt and feeling of unease is the thin thread back to who we really are, the indigenous swan within us. This uneasiness is not simple to follow, it can lead to despair, great loneliness, and yet we must go there. It is only when we accept we are unhappy, when we become desperate, we actually start to re-connect to our soul. This may take many years and can be a hugely dark time. However, it can be worth it in the end.

The Elders

When we have found who we need to be, we become elders. These are those rare and beautiful beings shining in a very particular way. Elders are men and women, indeed right now it feels like there are a great deal more women elders out there than men. They are not necessarily ancient or very old, they are not found only in far away places, they live amongst us, but are often unseen or unnoticed. An elder has been through the accumulation and gathering phase, and is now prepared and seeking to off-load, to give away, his knowledge, to share it with the next generation. When I was in my early 30's, I stood on the banks of the River Severn near Gloucester, early in the morning, and watched as the Severn Bore approached. A freak wave surging up the river against the flow. Afterwards I talked about what I had seen with an elder, and he observed how I had led my life like the first peak of the wave -the point from which the wave came. I liked to lead from the front, to draw others into my wake, such behaviour was expected and commonplace, but then he thought for a little while.

He quietly added

"Maybe some day you'll learn how to lead from the back as well".

An elder knows and has experienced both ways.

For me the solution to the problem with teenagers lies in the creation of elders. The problem isn't the child, or even the child's parents…it's the child's grandparents! *Where are they? Are they involved in the child's life?* If we can actively involve them in the teenager's lives we stand a chance of affecting real change. The culture and society we are creating doesn't encourage such behaviour, and it will take a great deal of courage and will-power for these elders to start this work. Our society has become stagnant and superficial, we need desperately to address some very deeply embedded problems at the heart of our culture.

The Chasm

There is a great chasm yawning wider and larger with each passing year in the centre of our culture. It is our superficiality, it is our belief that material goods provide happiness, it is our focus on celebrity, it is our reliance on squared warmth. We are living in a fog of fear, loneliness, laziness, where we blame others and refuse to take responsibility. This has been created by our forgetting about the true nature of community, our inter-connectedness with each other, and all the other species on the planet. This is compounded by our lack of time, commitment and trust. Started by our loss of ritual and ceremony, our disconnection to grief, joy, celebration and wildness. Created by our forgetting about spirit, nature, the unknown, the impossible, about the things that really matter. We are not conscious of this great hole until we rub up against it, or fall into it. We do this when we loose a relative or someone we love, when we feel pain, true love, joy, when we remember how it feels to be alive, so many different ways. When we become aware of the great chasm, we panic, overawed by the immensity of it all. *Where do I start? What difference can I make?* I don't know the answers to those questions, we all have a different gifts to bring. All I know is there are no short cuts. Our culture is built on a by-pass constructed by our intention to avoid feeling anything at all costs. We are attempting to by-pass the great chasm, and as the chasm expands and increases, we are making longer and longer short cuts to avoid the obvious.

There are no simple short-term solutions to the troubles we presently face. I was recently asked by a colleague to come up with some policy statements for the Welsh Assembly Government on teenagers. As we discussed each stage of the solutions it became obvious they could not be used as general statements. They relied on local solutions, based on local resources, so each would need to be different. They also depended on a community commitment well beyond just teenagers, and this would cut across governmental departments and responsibilities, making them unenforceable. This is the length and depth of our present problem, and the sooner we come to terms with it, the better. The long-term solutions involve the whole community, they involve commitment, training, expertise, experimentation, beyond the limits of our present culture. I know I am not alone in thinking this, there are many people all coming to same conclusions, and I know we will create viable and worthwhile solutions....we have to.

Maleness

Please women, mothers and grandmothers repeat after me......*"Men are lovely"* I know there are rank bastards out there, please don't let them cloud the picture. Women need men to be proper men. We all need initiated men. Mothers who have boys need positive male role models. Mothers who have girls need positive male role models. Men do not have to be cruel, do not have to unfeeling, do not have to be hard, do not have to use violence. If I can change one aspect of today's culture, it would be this. I am seeking to change these messages, and they are deeply ingrained. To be a man you can cry, to be a man you can love. Both men and women need to look long and hard at this. I work with some of the last miners in South Wales, and it is a real privilege to be with them. I am jealous of the strength and depth of the bonds of friendship they have formed. They are truly initiated men who have formed life long friendships and treat each other with respect. I have had a similar experience with the fire brigade. Men form incredibly sensitive and caring relationships amongst themselves.

Men are very complex, *please don't laugh*. They go through a wide range of complex changes in their lives and this needs to be honoured and understood. In the thirty years I've worked with men I have had the privilege of working with babies, children, teenagers, fathers, gay men, grandfathers, great grandfathers, white, black, red, yellow, brown, all colours, all of whom have been complex and beautiful. I teach fathers and men about their relationship with their children, and I encourage them to think lovingly and caringly about their kids. I do this work in some of the most severely deprived communities in Britain and Europe. These men can form and develop beautifully supportive relationships with their children, and this gives us all hope. They are flying in the face of their parenting, and how their parents were parented. They are creating a new precedent of which I am extremely proud, they are re-learning what it is to be a man. This book is a small step towards understanding and recognizing that emerging new maleness.

The Ugly Duckling
The one outstanding person in my field is Robert Bly. His starting points are the ancient myths, the stories of the land. The interpretation of myths, nursery rhymes, and legends as archetypes and personal stories. I sought to examine my own cultural background and see what lay there as resources. I looked at ancient texts - the *Mabinogion*, the Norse legends - but found them too removed. Too many long and confusing names to remember. I looked at more modern tales, and was drawn to *'The Ugly Duckling'* by Hans Christian Andersen. I thought it was a story about the artist, the misfit in society, and identified strongly with it. I wanted to use it as a teaching tool with groups, but it has been mis-translated, abused, and distorted for many years. Then I was able to gain access to a recent translation of the story- as close to the original as you can get. I gained the story through Rosie Beech, and would like to thank her for sending it to me. When I first read it I cried - at the beauty of his words, his ability to describe poetically anguish and despair. I cried for the pain carried in the story, the depth of the emotional trauma, his stand against bullies, and his understanding of loneliness. I realized the story is not just about the misfit artist, it is about a boy with an absent father. It is a story so pertinent and relevant to our times, it needs to be examined, and re-read in this modern context.

I will try to keep this book simple, when I say "I" it is my experience, when I say "we" it will refer to a Western European or American standpoint. When I state specific ages, like 56, they are just my interpretations, they do not have to apply to you. I share *The Ugly Duckling* with fathers, men and boys, and mixed groups as well. We take turns telling it, we discussed the relevance it has to each of us. Every time I read it I appreciate another aspect of the story. Every time, my perception shifts, I become more aware of myself, the relevance of the story to modern life, and it's bearing on the work I am involved in. I wanted to write down the interpretations and views that have arisen from it in the hope others will find them of value. I know this process has been very transformative, cathartic for me, and many other people. So, I pass this on with love and blessings to you all.

CHAPTER ONE
THE UGLY DUCKLING
by Hans Christian Andersen

It was so beautiful out in the country. It was summer. The oats were still green, but the wheat was turning yellow. Down in the meadow the grass had been cut and made into haystacks; and there the storks walked on their long red legs talking Egyptian, because that was the language they had been taught by their mothers. The fields were enclosed by woods, and hidden among them were little lakes and pools. Yes, it certainly was lovely out there in the country!

The old castle, with its deep moat surrounding it, lay bathed in sunshine. Between the heavy walls and the edge of the moat there was a narrow strip of land covered by a whole forest of burdock plants. Their leaves were large and some of the stalks were so tall that a child could stand upright under them and imagine that he was in the middle of the wild and lonesome woods. Here a duck had built her nest. While she sat waiting for the eggs to hatch, she felt a little sorry for herself because it was taking so long and hardly anybody came to visit her. The other ducks preferred swimming in the moat to sitting under a dock leaf and gossiping.

Finally the eggs began to crack. "Peep …Peep" they said one after another. The egg yolks had become alive and were sticking out their heads.

"Quack…Quack.." said their mother. "Look around you."

And the ducklings did; they glanced at the green world about them, and that was what their mother wanted them to do, for green was good for their eyes.

"How big the world is!" piped the little ones, for they had much more space to move around in now than they had had inside the egg.

"Do you think that this is the whole world?" quacked their mother. "The world is much larger than this. It stretches as far as the minister's wheat fields, though I have not been there …Are you all here?" The duck got up and turned around to look at her nest. "Oh no, the biggest egg hasn't hatched yet; and I'm so tired of sitting here! I wonder how long it will take?" she wailed, and sat down again.

"What's new?" asked an old duck who had come visiting.

"One of the eggs is taking so long" complained the mother duck. "It won't crack. But take a look at the others. They are the sweetest little ducklings you have ever seen; and every one of them looks exactly like their father. That scoundrel hasn't come to visit me once."

"Let me look at the egg that won't hatch," demanded the old duck. "I am sure that it's a turkey egg! I was fooled that way once. You can't imagine what it's like. Turkeys are afraid of the water. I couldn't get them to go into it. I quacked and I nipped them, but nothing helped. Let me see that egg! …Yes, it's a turkey egg. Just let it lie there. You go and teach your young ones how to swim, that's my advice."

"I have sat on it so long that I guess I can sit a little longer, at least until they get the hay in." replied the mother duck.

"Suit yourself." said the older duck, and went on.

At last the big egg cracked too. "Peep ... Peep" said the young one, and tumbled out. He was big and very ugly.

The mother duck looked at him. "He's awfully big for his age," she said. "He doesn't look like any of the others. I wonder if he could be a turkey? Well, we shall soon see. Into the water he will go, even if I have to kick him to make him do it."

The next day the weather was gloriously beautiful. The sun shone on the forest of burdock plants. The mother duck took her whole brood to the moat. "Quack ... Quack.." she ordered.

One after the other, the little ducklings plunged into the water. For a moment their heads disappeared, but then they popped up again and the little ones floated like so many corks. Their legs knew what to do without being told. All of the new brood swam very nicely, even the ugly one.

"He is no turkey" mumbled the mother. "See how beautifully he uses his legs and how straight he holds his neck. He is my own child and, when you look closely at him, he's quite handsome... Quack! Quack! Follow me and I'll take you to the henyard and introduce you to everyone. But stay close to me, so that no one steps on you, and look out for the cat."

They heard an awful noise when they arrived at the henyard. Two families of ducks had got into a fight over the head of an eel. Neither of them got it, for it was swiped by the cat.

"That is the way of the world," said the mother duck, and licked her bill. She would have liked to have the eel's head herself. "Walk nicely" she admonished them. "And remember to bow to the old duck over there. She has Spanish blood in her veins and is the most aristocratic fowl here. That is why she is so fat and has a red rag tied around one of her legs. That is the highest mark of distinction a duck can be given. It means so much that she will never be done away with; and all the other fowl and the human beings know who she is. Quack! Quack!... Don't walk, waddle like well-brought-up ducklings. Keep your legs far apart, just as your mother and father have always done. Bow your heads and say, Quack!" And that was what the little ducklings did.

Other ducks gathered about them and said loudly, "What do we want that gang here for? Aren't there enough of us already? Pooh! Look how ugly one of them is! He's the last straw!" And one of the ducks flew over and bit the ugly duckling on the neck.

"Leave him alone!" shouted the mother. "He hasn't done anyone any harm."

"He's big and he doesn't look like everybody else!" replied the duck who had bitten him. "And that's reason enough to beat him."

"Very good-looking children you have," remarked the duck with the red rag around one of her legs. "All of them are beautiful except one. He didn't turn out very well. I wish you could make him over again."

"That's not possible, Your Grace," answered the mother duck. "He may not be handsome, but he has a good character and swims as well as the others, if not a little better.

Perhaps he will grow handsomer as he grows older and becomes a bit smaller. He was in the egg too long, and that is why he doesn't have the right shape." She smoothed his neck for a moment and then added, "Besides, he's a drake; and it doesn't matter so much what he looks like. He is strong and I am sure he will be able to take care of himself."

"Well, the others are nice," said the old duck. "Make yourself at home, and if you should find an eel's head, you may bring it to me."

And they were "at home."

The poor little duckling, who had been the last to hatch and was so ugly, was bitten and pushed and made fun of both by the hens and by the other ducks. The turkey cock (who had been born with spurs on, and therefore thought he was an emperor) rustled his feathers as if he were a full-rigged ship under sail, and strutted up to the duckling. He gobbled so loudly at him that his own face got all red.

The poor little duckling did not know where to turn. How he grieved over his ugliness, and how sad he was! The poor creature was mocked and laughed at by the whole henyard.

That was the first day; and each day that followed was worse than the one before. The poor duckling was chased and mistreated by everyone, even his own sisters and brothers, who quacked again and again, "If only the cat would get you, you ugly thing!"

Even his mother said, "I wish you were far away." The other ducks bit him and the hens pecked at him. The little girl who came to feed the fowls kicked him.

At last the duckling ran away. He flew over the tops of the bushes, frightening all the little birds so that they flew up into the air. "They, too, think I am ugly." Thought the duckling, and closed his eyes – but he kept on running.

Finally he came to a great swamp where wild ducks lived; and here he stayed for the night, for he was too tired to go any farther.

In the morning he was discovered by the wild ducks. They looked at him and one of them asked, "What kind of bird are you?"

The ugly duckling bowed in all directions, for he was trying to be as polite as he knew how.

"You are ugly," said the wild ducks, "but that is no concern of ours, as long as you don't try to marry into our family."

The poor duckling wasn't thinking of marriage. All he wanted was to be allowed to swim among the reeds and drink a little water when he was thirsty.

He spent two days in the swamp; then two wild geese came – or rather, two wild ganders, for they were males. They had been hatched not long ago; therefore they were both frank and bold.

"Listen, comrade," they said. "You are so ugly that we like you. Do you want to migrate with us? Not far from here there is a marsh where some beautiful wild geese live. They are all lovely maidens, and you are so ugly that you may seek your fortune among them. Come along."

"Bang! Bang!" Two shots were heard and both the ganders fell down dead among the reeds, and the water turned red from their blood.

"Bang! Bang!" Again came the sound of shots, and a flock of wild geese flew up.

The whole swamp was surrounded by hunters; from every direction came the awful noise. Some of the hunters had hidden behind bushes or among the reeds but others, screened from sight by the leaves, sat on the long, low branches of the trees that stretched out over the swamp. The blue smoke from the guns lay like a fog over the water and among the trees. Dogs came splashing through the marsh, and they bent and broke the reeds.

The poor little duckling was terrified. He was about to tuck his head under his wing, in order to hide, when he saw a big dog peering at him through the reeds. The dog's tongue hung out of its mouth and its eyes glistened evilly. It bared its teeth. Splash! It turned away without touching the duckling.

"Oh, thank God!" he sighed. "I am so ugly that even the dog doesn't want to bite me."

The little duckling lay as still as he could while the shots whistled through the reeds. Not until the middle of the afternoon did the shooting stop; but the poor little duckling was still so frightened that he waited several hours longer before taking his head out from under his wing. The he ran as quickly as he could out of the swamp. Across the fields and meadows he went, but a wind had come up and he found it hard to make his way against it.

Toward evening he came upon a poor little hut. It was so wretchedly crooked that it looked as if it couldn't make up its mind which way to fall and that was why it was still standing. The wind was blowing so hard that the poor little duckling had to sit down in order not to be blown away. Suddenly he noticed that the door was off its hinges, making a crack; and he squeezed himself through it and was inside.

An old woman lived in the hut with her cat and her hen. The cat was called Sonny and could both arch his back and purr. Oh yes, he could also make sparks if you rubbed his fur the wrong way. The hen had very short legs and that was why she was called Cluck Lowlegs. But she was good at laying eggs, and the old woman loved her as if she were her own child.

In the morning the hen and the cat discovered the duckling. The cat meowed and the hen clucked.

"What is going on?" asked the old woman, and looked around. She couldn't see very well, and when she found the duckling she thought it was a fat, full-grown duck. "What a fine catch!" she exclaimed, "Now we shall have duck eggs, unless it's a drake. We'll give it a try."

So the duckling was allowed to stay for three weeks on probation, but he laid no eggs. The cat was master of the house and the hen the mistress. They always referred to themselves as "we and the world," for they thought that they were half the world - and the better half at that. The duckling thought that he should be allowed to have a different opinion, but the hen did not agree.

"Can you lay eggs?" she demanded.

"No." answered the duckling.

"Then keep your mouth shut."

And the cat asked, "Can you arch your back? Can you purr? Can you make sparks?"

"No."

"Well, in that case, you have no right to have an opinion when sensible people are talking."

The duckling was sitting in the corner and was in a bad mood. Suddenly he recalled how lovely it could be outside in the fresh air when the sun shone; a great longing to be floating in the water came over the duckling, and he could not help talking about it.

"What is the matter with you?" asked the hen as soon as she had heard what he had to say. "You have nothing to do, that's why you get ideas like that. Lay eggs or purr, and such notions will disappear."

"You have no idea how delightful it is to float in the water, and to dive down to the bottom of a lake and get your head wet." said the duckling.

"Yes, that certainly does sound amusing," said the hen. "You must have gone mad. Ask the cat - he is the most intelligent being I know - ask him whether he likes to swim or dive down to the bottom of a lake. Don't take my word for anything ... Ask the old woman, who is the cleverest person in the world; ask her whether she likes to float and to get her head all wet."

"You don't understand me!" wailed the duckling.

"And if I don't understand you, who will? I hope you don't think that you are wiser than the cat or the old woman - not to mention myself. Don't give yourself airs! Thank your Creator for all He has done for you. Aren't you sitting in a warm room among intelligent people whom you could learn something from? While you, yourself, do nothing but say a lot of nonsense and aren't the least bit amusing! Believe me, that's the truth, and I am only telling it to you for your own good. That's how you recognize a true friend; it's someone who is willing to tell you the truth, no matter how unpleasant it is. Now get to work: lay some eggs, or learn to purr and arch your back."

"I think I'll go out into the wide world." replied the duckling.

"Go right ahead!" said the hen.

And the duckling left. He found a lake where he could float in the water and dive to the bottom. There were other ducks, but they ignored him because he was so ugly.

Autumn came and the leaves turned yellow and brown, then they fell from the trees. The wind caught them and made them dance. The clouds were heavy with hail and snow. A raven sat on a fence and screeched, "Ach! Ach!" because it was so cold. When just thinking of how cold it was is enough to make one shiver, what a terrible time the duckling must have had.

One evening just as the sun was setting gloriously, a flock of beautiful birds came out from among the rushes. Their feathers were so white that they glistened; and they had long, graceful necks. They were swans. They made a very loud cry, then they spread their powerful wings. They were flying south to a warmer climate, where the lakes were not frozen in the winter. Higher and higher they circled. The ugly duckling turned round and round in the water like a wheel and stretched his neck up toward the sky; he felt a strange longing. He screeched so piercingly that he frightened himself.

Oh, he would never forget those beautiful birds, those happy birds. When they were out of sight the duckling dived down under the water to the bottom of the lake; and when he came up again he was beside himself. He did not know the name of those birds or where they were going, and yet he felt that he loved them as he had never loved any other creatures. He did not envy them. It did not even occur to him to wish that he were so handsome himself. He would have been happy if the other ducks had let him stay in the henyard: that poor, ugly bird!

The weather grew colder and colder. The duckling had to swim round and round in the water, to keep just a little space for himself that wasn't frozen. Each night his hole became smaller and smaller. On all sides of him the ice creaked and groaned. The little duckling had to keep his feet constantly in motion so that the last bit of open water wouldn't become ice. At last he was too tired to swim any more. He sat still. The ice closed in around him and he was frozen fast.

Early the next morning a farmer saw him and with his clogs broke the ice to free the duckling. The man put the bird under his arm and took it home to his wife, who brought the duckling back to life.

The children wanted to play with him. But the duckling was afraid that they were going to hurt him, so he flapped his wings and flew right into the milk pail. From there he flew into a big bowl of butter and then into a barrel of flour. What a sight he was!

The farmer's wife yelled and chased him with a poker. The children laughed and almost fell on top of each other, trying to catch him; and how they screamed! Luckily for the duckling, the door was open. He got out of the house and found a hiding place beneath some bushes, in the newly fallen snow; and there he lay so still, as though there were hardly any life left in him.

It would be too horrible to tell of all the hardship and suffering the duckling experienced that long winter. It is enough to know that he did survive. When again the sun shone warmly and the larks began to sing, the duckling was lying among the reeds in the swamp. Spring had come!

He spread out his wings to fly. How strong and powerful they were! Before he knew it, he was far from the swamp and flying above a beautiful garden. The apple trees were blooming and the lilac bushes stretched their flower-covered branches over the water of a winding canal. Everything was so beautiful: so fresh and green. Out of a forest of rushes came three swans. They ruffled their feathers and floated so lightly on the water. The ugly duckling recognized the birds and felt again that strange sadness come over him.

"I shall fly over to them, those royal birds! And they can hack me to death because I, who am so ugly, dare to approach them! What difference does it make? It is better to be killed by them than to be bitten by the other ducks, and pecked by the hens, and kicked by the girl who tends the henyard; or to suffer through the winter."

And he lighted on the water and swam toward the magnificent swans. When they saw him they ruffled their feathers and started to swim in his direction. They were coming to meet him.

"Kill me," whispered the poor creature, and bent his head humbly while he waited for death. But what was that he saw in the water? It was his own reflection; and he was no longer an awkward, clumsy, grey bird, so ungainly and so ugly. He was a swan!

It does not matter that one has been born in the henyard as long as one has lain in a swan's egg.

He was thankful that he had known so much want, and gone through so much suffering, for it made him appreciate his present happiness and the loveliness of everything about him all the more. The swans made a circle around him and caressed him with their beaks.

Some children came out into the garden. They had brought bread with them to feed the swans. The youngest child shouted, "Look, there's a new one!" All the children joyfully clapped their hands, and they ran to tell their parents. Cake and bread were cast on the water for the swans. Everyone agreed that the new swan was the most beautiful of them all. The older swans bowed towards him.

He felt so shy that he hid his head beneath his wing. He was too happy, but not proud, for a kind heart can never be proud. He thought of the time when he had been mocked and persecuted. And now everyone said that he was the most beautiful of the most beautiful birds. And the lilac bushes stretched their branches right down to the water for him. The sun shone so warm and brightly. He ruffled his feathers and raised his slender neck, while out of the joy in his heart, he thought, "Such happiness I did not dream of when I was the ugly duckling."

CHAPTER TWO
THE RELEVANCE OF THE UGLY DUCKLING

I know you are all familiar with the story, but I hope you have taken the time to read it again, to appreciate how very complex, dark, and moving the tale is. It must have been written as a form of therapy, it closely follows the author's life story. Hans Christian Andersen was a single parent child and experienced a great deal of trauma before he was able to make a living as a writer. He pre-dates Freud, he died in Freud's twentieth year, but I believe this tale has to be personal. As an individual he was able to gain fame and fortune from being an author and storyteller, and I am sure along the way many people tried to dissuade him from such a path.

I want to use the story to tell two concurrent themes:-

The first relates to the transformative experiences the Ugly Duckling encounters from the time he leaves the farmyard through to the end of the story. For me, he is a teenager, and his experiences are typical for most of our young people today. I will use them to describe a rite of passage for a boy without a father or a male role model. I will also add details in terms of the way this experience could have been changed if the Ugly Duckling had a mentor guiding him.

The second relates these experiences to all of us - men and women. His journey from egg to swan takes just a year, but I believe it describes a much longer passage of time. The tale tells us how to follow our heart, how to find out what we are truly worth and pursue it. The Ugly Duckling (Hans Christian Andersen) is a good example of someone coming through adversity to eventually find himself. It shows how we can all become mature, at peace, gain self-confident. In both cases the story relates to a rite of passage.

Rites of passage

Everyone seems to be talking about them, it has become quite a familiar phrase - it used to lurk only in new age discussions or shamanic texts. In my terms it is:-

* *a crisis, and the admission of such*
* *allied to a test of yourself*
* *connecting to your 'souls purpose'*
* *leading to the creation of a 'new' person*
* *all of which is held by elders*

These five elements are the keys. Our indigenous ancestors knew all about them, they performed such rituals on every continent of the planet for thousands of years. Every indigenous people had rites of passage ceremonies and rituals, not just for teenagers, but at other stages in life as well. When someone became a parent; when they became a grandparent; when they became an elder. At each of these times there was a need for a rite of passage, for guidance to be given in order for the individual to come through the crisis or event. They were aware of the true nature of any such life crisis – *it is a phase you go through - it isn't permanent.*

A rite of passage is by its nature hard – it's not the easy or soft option. This is reality, not virtual reality! During the rite we seek help, we are assisted, and this creates bonds - these links can become permanent, they can last a long time. When we do this properly - we create society - we create community. When we have been initiated we can take our rightful places in society.

Our present culture, our way of being, is very recent. We haven't always been this superficial, scratch our skin, the indigenous knowledge is still there, just below the surface. Even as recently as during the industrial revolution we were still creating rites of passage for teenage boys - *what do you think apprenticeships in the coal and steel industries were?* When we have been assisted through such a rite of passage we become 'safe'. As individuals we become content in the knowledge of who we are, what we do, and our role within society. When we connect to our souls' purpose we can contribute wholeheartedly to the well being of others. A great many people living today have not received or been part of such work. When you don't do it, you can remain immature, insensitive, selfish, and unable to really help anyone else. We need this wisdom right here and right now, as a matter of urgency. At least three, if not more, generations haven't found their soul's purpose. As each generation passes this need increases, as a people we become disconsolate, always looking outside ourselves for the answers, feeling we are alone.

*"Whatever your age, whatever your work, whether you are married or single, male or female, of modest means or fabulously rich, something is missing in your life. You may not know exactly what it is. You may not be able to define it. You are aware only that the need to find that elusive 'something' has been with you for a very long time."*1*

Such feelings affect all of us at some time in our lives. You are not alone, hopefully, this book will remind you to re-connect to who you really are. As I said there are two themes in the book, please don't think just because you don't have a teenage child, or are not a teenager, the lessons don't apply to you.

The journey described in the Ugly Duckling seems very dangerous and fraught at times, but is also rewarding and worthwhile. He, like so many young people, must take this path. He had no viable male role models who might be able to show him another way. He seeks and eventually finds elders who recognize and honour him. His journey could have been less perilous if he'd had elders to guide him, but there again it might not. My work has led me to the conclusion that younger men need older men to mentor and assist them through their adolescence and beyond. They are the missing links enabling a boy to become a man, and I will elucidate on this throughout the book. I know in my bones this represents a truth, but I am not going to insist everyone has to be put through rites of passage by elders. I don't believe in compunction or there being only one way. We are all doing the work, consciously or unconsciously. The Ugly Duckling arrives at a place of eldership eventually.

Elders

I will use this term throughout the book, for me, it represents someone who has experienced a great deal of life. Possibly they are over the age of 56. Someone, who is no longer caring for young children. Someone who has distilled knowledge into wisdom. Someone who has a knowing look in their eye. Someone who has the scars to prove it, but doesn't need to show them! Someone who quite possibly was a lot of trouble in younger days. A lot of the boys who are 'causing us trouble' right now will become mature and well liked elders, however, they will need support, and there will be trauma and drama along the way. Almost invariably, the troublesome young people become the most worthwhile adults, given the chance. As a society we need to remember this and become so accommodating as to give them the chance.

Too many people think the best times lie in our past- some believe we need to revert to a hunter gathering existence; some believe we were better off when we had the discipline and violence of the Victorian era; some have an idealized view of the late '40s and '50s as being a 'golden era' of respect and trust. There is no way back. There is only the future. That is my interest. If I can use stories and experiences from the past to illustrate and give ideas to people for the future, then so be it. I give examples from indigenous people around the world, they connect us back to our lost past. But, please don't think I believe the past is better than the future. Many of our present problems arise from people having a misguided belief about the past being better than the present. I am seeking to make my life, my children's lives, and my children's children's lives better and more fulfilled.

The next chapters
In order for you to be able to use this book easily, each of the chapters is divided into the following sections:-

The Story - a small section of the Ugly Duckling

Interpretation of this part of the story – my personal views

Resonance for us now – the bigger picture

Examples from near and far – the ways in which others have worked with these ideas

How can we use this? – ideas and thoughts on how to incorporate this into our lives and how to become elders.

CHAPTER THREE
KNOWERS OF NATURE

The Story

"It was so beautiful out in the country. It was summer. The oats were still green, but the wheat was turning yellow. Down in the meadow the grass had been cut and made into haystacks; and there the storks walked on their long red legs talking Egyptian, because that was the language they had been taught by their mothers. The fields were enclosed by woods, and hidden among them were little lakes and pools. Yes, it certainly was lovely out there in the country!"

Interpretation of this part of the story

"Whatever being comes to be,
Be it motionless or moving,
Derives its being from the union
Of 'field' and 'knower of field' - this know."
Bhagavad-gita, xiii, 26

Hans Christian Andersen shows a wonderful understanding of nature, the identification of the time of year, not by its month, but by the colour of oats and wheat. All you need to know is it is summer, a time of light, birth and vigour. Nature is the source of the story, it is about birds, and yet it is well within our human capabilities to read nature in the ways animals do. Indeed, it can be through such a close connection to nature we start to understand our own lives. The connected-ness of the author to nature and his appreciation of it, have given him the ability to tell the story in such a mystical and appropriate manner. This awareness is sadly lacking in today's Western culture, and it is just a little hint towards the depth and wisdom within a love of nature, which can only come from close observation and intimacy. It is a hint about how old the story is, how ancient the roots of the words are. We need to be a *'knower of field'* and the only way to do that is to spend time in the field. In the groups I have worked with, many comment on this opening passage as making them feel all warm inside, and on hearing it, being able to see the green and golden flow of the crops. It is almost a collective memory imprinted in our minds, representing a peace and wholeness often lacking in our lives.

Resonance for us now

Many people feel they don't live in nature, many people feel they have isolated themselves from the natural world, *'you have to live in the country to understand nature'*. To be blunt, this is untrue. Obviously, if you live in a rural idyll, and have the time to spend hours and days in it, you can be close to nature. But, there are many people I know who live in the country who are incredibly out of touch with nature. Equally, there are many people I know who live in large cities, who are fantastically in touch with nature. To be in touch with nature, I believe, you need to see everything as part of it. You don't have to be in the wilderness to be in nature, you are equally surrounded by it in a tower block. Nature is human, we are natural, there is no separation. We are always in nature wherever we are. Although I was brought up in London, my brother imbued me with a love of birds. He was forever seeking out birds and observing them from a very young age. My debt to my brother is I can be anywhere in Britain and know what birds are singing, what birds are passing glimpses in the bushes. I know their names because of the hours and days spent as a boy observing, and when I try to explain how I know it is very difficult. I just do.

Being in nature is one thing, knowing nature is another. The observation and interpretation of natural phenomenon is innate in all of us. We are fascinated by our surroundings and we are always observing and interpreting them. Watching your favourite soap on television is an observation of nature. When we are absorbed, we are observing *'what does she mean by that? Will he really go out with her?'* When we ask ourselves these questions, it's an indication we are observing nature. The internal answers *'I'm sure he really fancies her'*, are the conclusions of a knower of nature. *'It's in the way he talks to her, it's in the way that he is always looking for her in the crowd.'*

Observation

If you want to understand and interact with the whole of nature, not just humans, it is easier to be in wilder, less populated, areas. By spending time in wilderness and the more rural areas, we feed our souls more easily. Being amongst wild things, be they animals, plants or places, there is a natural absorption of harmony, well-being, and a sense of correctness. That's why we all enjoy going on holiday and lying in the sun. When we do this, we need to start from a point of observing it, not making judgments. To be an observer is an intuitive skill, children are very good at observing, indeed, that is their primary means of learning. As we grow older we become more judgmental and we seek to interpret our surroundings. I believe we need to passively observe more often. Non-judgmental observation is a very absorbing and delightful state to be in. It links us into a state of mind which is the same as all those eastern practices of meditation and physical activities – Yoga, Tai Chi, etc –. Being in nature and being an observer is simple and yet very profound. To be with yourself, rather than distracting yourself through other things, is the ideal. The more you do this, the easier it will become. If you do it often or deeply enough, you will observe mysterious events, different to the expected, which take you by surprise and cause unexpected reactions. These may be the quality of light on clouds near sunset, the dancing shapes of starlings in the winter as they settling to roost, the waving celebration of summer that is a field of barley, twinkling and shimmering in the sun. These experiences create wonder in us. In those moments, we may cry unexpectedly, or smile, shout out loud just for the sake of it. All of us can benefit hugely from such mystical experiences in our lives. When we have them, they lead us to question our reality, they stretch us and paradoxically make us feel more complete.

When confronted by things we don't know or understand it is also intuitive to want to interpret them. This is fine, it is a natural progression. We need to use our accumulated knowledge and wisdom to interpret these occurrences or phenomenon. But, don't be in too much of a hurry. Spend time just looking. The combination of observation and the interpretation of nature nurtures wisdom, but it takes time, experience and knowledge, something only a few us of have achieved. Hans Christian Andersen knew about all this, he was a very good observer of nature, and he used his skills to then create images and wonderfully imaginative interpretations. *"...the storks walking on their long red legs talking Egyptian, because that was the language they had been taught by their mothers."* Is just such a beautifully poetic description of storks. It imbues them with mystery and awe, as anyone who has seen storks will identify. Storks are exotic, they seem so out of place in lowland Denmark, it is no wonder they speak Egyptian, as they are so different. Their language is the language of their winter retreat, where they fly, and is a little reminder of the journeys most of the characters are due to make.

Examples from near and far

His description of the landscape also reflects an innate love of that particular land, this comes from a sense of belonging to his place, Denmark. This was intuitive in so many people before the industrial revolution. We all knew where we were in the world, and how good our place felt.

"The Crow country is a good country. The Great Spirit put it exactly in the right place; while you are in it you fare well; whenever you are out of it, whichever way you travel, you fare worse...The Crow country is exactly in the right place. Everything good is to be found there. There is no place like Crow country."

This is a quote from Arapooish, a leader of the Crow Indians of Montana in 1837, just 7 years before Hans Christian Andersen wrote the Ugly Duckling. They both reflect a genuine love of their land, and within this love lies the history of the land, respect for the nature of the land, and a knowledge this relationship is thousands of years old. In 1844 the great majority of people on the planet felt this way about their land. They were intimately connected to their place and they knew how to be in harmony with the seasons and the land. Only a tiny percentage of people had been infected by the contagious diseases of materialism and celebrity. How times have changed in less than two hundred years!

How can we use this?
On a personal level

We are natural, as an individual you are part of nature, you are carrying inside you natural elements.

As a knower of nature, you need to know yourself.

This can start with not putting so many poisons into your body, stopping the pollution of your body.

Take time to breath, learn how to breath correctly.

By doing this you will be appreciating the innate beauty of your own nature.

These things will make you happier, healthier, and prolonging your life.

When you breath correctly you will start to be able to let go of thoughts, quieten the voices in your head.

Take time to just observe things, don't judge them, just let them happen.

Try to learn the names of plants, trees, birds, those things in nature that interest you, don't force yourself, if it is not of interest to you.

Once you know the name of something, observe it's character. For instance, once you know what a chaffinch looks like, observe what it does, where it sits in the trees, how it cocks it's head, how it flies.

Admire the innate sense of chaffinch-ness that all chaffinches have!

If we are to become elders

We need to share this knowledge and enthusiasm with children and teenagers. When someone really enjoys being in nature, they can inspire others to do the same. When we role model our enthusiasm we become attractive, especially to children and younger people. Don't keep your enthusiasm to yourself. Share it with your children and with other children.

Take the children out into the park and try to identify the different species of birds, plants, trees you find, try to find more each trip, it needs to be fun, but also a challenge. Men are particularly good at this, observing and collating – that's why the vast majority of train spotters and bird watchers are male. Taking this to another stage, men are good at trips out, going on adventures. They can take children fishing, out on boats, surfing, camping, hiking in the woods, making dens, cooking over an open fire. Such activities are hugely important for children, and they develop their understanding of themselves. This is equally important for girls as well as boys. They need to see men being enthusiastic and challenged, don't we all!

If you don't think you can do this, then seek training and experience. Try out the activities for yourself first, see what happens, or go on some training courses. Outdoor and wilderness pursuits are now very popular, and there are courses, training and development programmes in a wide range of skills. Wilderness survival, climbing, orienteering, the list is endless. By receiving such training you will be learning about yourself, increasing your confidence, and you will be able to share this with the next generations. This is vital work.

CHAPTER FOUR
STORYTELLING

The Story

       "The old castle, with its deep moat surrounding it, lay bathed in sunshine. Between the heavy walls and the edge of the moat there was a narrow strip of land covered by a whole forest of burdock plants. Their leaves were large and some of the stalks were so tall that a child could stand upright under them and imagine that he was in the middle of the wild and lonesome woods. Here a duck had built her nest. While she sat waiting for the eggs to hatch, she felt a little sorry for herself because it was taking so long and hardly anybody came to visit her. The other ducks preferred swimming in the moat to sitting under a dock leaf and gossiping."

Interpretation of this part of the story

This passage humanizes the story, the old castle, the size of a child, all let us know the story is about us, even the duck is humanized, enabling us to understand this is metaphor. Ducks don't feel sorry for themselves, they don't gossip, humans do. It is the start of a gorgeous story, which is full of detail and richly textured descriptions.

Resonance for us now

This story becomes a beautiful thing in it's own right. It is also, quite a magical and mysterious phenomenon. It contains hidden depths and meanings, which I hope to tease out over the next pages. It is a story for telling, re-telling, and especially for telling out loud. The poetic rhythm of the words are suited to sitting round a fire, or being in a circle. It needs to be read and shared with others.

The content of the story is quite shocking on occasions, it is a dark tale, but it is relevant to everyone. It is a story for grown ups as well as for children, it is about all of us. It is an ancient story and in those ancient stories they didn't hold back from the truth. Those kinds of stories were told to everyone in the community and the children gained what they needed from hearing them. I believe there is no reason for us to protect children from stories of hardship and death. These stories have vital lessons built into them, and when we 'artificially sweeten' them they loose a huge amount of power and creativity. Children intuitively don't want such sweetened stories, they seek the real thing, and are very happy to be scared and impressed by stories. They gain what they need at the relevant times during their lives. Just like the rest of us.

Examples from near and far

There are too many to number here!

How can we use this?

On a personal level

Innate in us all is a storyteller.

Our genes are programmed to expect spending a large amount of the day being sociable and collaborating with others. We are sociable beasts, seeking company and friendship. However solitary we think we are, however self-reliant we believe ourselves to be, it is not intuitive.

- ★ We all need to practice telling stories, sharing them with others.
- ★ We all know stories that will fascinate and transfix other people by their telling. They are our own stories.
- ★ We all need to tell our own stories, it is part of growing up, becoming mature. The older you become the more important it is to share your story. Not in an egotistic way, but as a service to others.
- ★ Not by believing your experience is more important than anyone else's, but knowing the next generation needs to hear it, in order for them to be able transcend it, go beyond it.

★　　　　　When you are interested in becoming a storyteller, you also develop a love of language. You expand and develop your vocabulary, and this helps to expand your mind.

★　　　　　All storytellers start by telling their stories to their peers. Their peers are good barometers, they can detect bull shit, and they deal with the truth.

★　　　　　Once you have become a good peer storyteller, you can then become a good cross-generational storyteller.

If we are to become elders

You need to be familiar with telling stories. Practice makes perfect. Tell stories to young children, they love wild and imaginative stuff. You can do this anywhere and at anytime. Tell stories to young adults and you have a very different challenge. I tell stories on a regular basis to groups of teenagers, street wise, hardened, toughened individuals, and that is quite a challenge. However, I tell those stories in the right circumstances, at night, round a campfire. I tell them in a way which draws them in, makes them feel afraid, makes them laugh, makes them cry. Something happens to a story when it is told at night in the open air. I've told the Ugly Duckling many times round a fire, and it moves and shocks teenagers every time.

You need to have some good stories to tell in the first place, so read lots of stories. Tell stories from different countries, from different traditions, they can come from so many different places. You need to remember quite how powerful stories can be. They can have an almost irresistible effect on people. I once told a particularly powerful story to a group of teenage school children in Eastern Germany, just after the wall came down. I told it to them so they could connect to the outside world, it came from South America. At a certain point the story becomes so laden with emotion that everyone cries, this just is the way of the story, and I felt it would be useful for them to experience this communal grief. I told the story, they cried, and then we moved through it. I looked round the room at the end and checked everyone was recovered, and suddenly realize one of the teachers had been in the room with us, despite my requested for no teachers to be present. I went to him and asked if he was alright, as I knew he must have cried, and this could have affected his relationship to the pupils. He was at peace, he said it was the first time he had ever cried in front of his pupils, but he felt it had been important for them to see it affecting him as well. Later, he said he came in because he wanted the challenge of sitting through the story and not crying, but he had failed! Such is the power of storytelling. As a storyteller you need to be flexible and adaptable. You need to know when to not tell stories as well as when to change them, in order to keep people attentive. It's a great skill, but it is one of the oldest and most innate of all our abilities. The same applies to singing, or making music, or doing arts and crafts. These are our basic tool kit for communication, they have been with us for thousands of years. If you are a master of one or some of them, then you will always find friendship and a welcome even amongst total strangers. Such is the power of being a storyteller.

CHAPTER FIVE
BOYS AND GIRLS

The Story

> *"Finally the eggs began to crack. "Peep ...Peep" they said one after another. The egg yolks had become alive and were sticking out their heads.*
> *"Quack...Quack.." said their mother. "Look around you."*
> *And the ducklings did; they glanced at the green world about them, and that was what their mother wanted them to do, for green was good for their eyes.*
> *"How big the world is!" piped the little ones, for they had much more space to move around in now than they had had inside the egg.*
> *"Do you think that this is the whole world?" quacked their mother. "The world is much larger than this. It stretches as far as the minister's wheat fields, though I have not been there .."*

Interpretation of this part of the story

These early eggs are female, as they hatch the mother imparts an important lesson...the world is big, but it stretches only so far. These are the domestic boundaries all mothers are in charge of, and she does this work intuitively. She gives them boundaries, *"as far as the Minister's wheat fields"*. Is that a discrete reference to religion? The Minister knows where the edge of existence is, his land reaches that far, no one else's does. The mother shows them where their place is in the world, and the edge of it is known, yet unexplored, as it is so far away. It is one of the most important lessons a child can receive from its parents – a definition of the safe and known world. This imparts a huge amount of security and a feeling of well being in the child. Your mother is the font of this knowledge. She confidently asserts the boundaries and limits, without doubt or uncertainty. However, she has imparted this message to the girls, and not the boy, he is not yet out of his shell. He hasn't heard the message. When he finally appears in the world, there will be no boundaries, there is no safety and security.

Resonance for us now

I work with a lot of boys on the council estates of South Wales. Boundary-less young men seeking a reaction, desperately seeking limits through their intimidatory behaviour. The single parent offspring with no role models who furtively seek boundaries, even though they don't know it. They seek them domestically at first, and then they go out into the wider world and pursue them. Throughout this time they don't feel held, so they don't feel respect. They feel limitless in their exponential seeking of boundaries. They manifest this in their addictions, their bullying, their callous brutality, and their mindlessly inconsiderate behaviour. Like most of those boys, the Ugly Duckling doesn't have a father, he has no role model to follow, so he has to make it up himself. How different it would have been if he had a father who cared, who knew what his job was around children.

Examples from near and far

In a sense, because we are no longer aware of the significance and importance of an extended family, we are now expecting far too much from the mothers and the fathers of our children. In the extended family the job of raising the boys and girls was

30

mainly performed by the grandparents. In the Dagara people of Ghana the responsibility lies with the grandfather to teach the boy about life, then he directs the boy back to his father. We lost this extended support structure for our children a long time ago, and it is a very difficult job to bring up children as a mother and a father, without support and caring helpers. Unfortunately, we don't expect our parents to only bring up children. We have created a culture in which success is measured by our children and the 'proper' jobs we do as well. We expect our mothers to not only nurture and love their children, but also to have a job, be sexual, keep young looks and figure, cook imaginatively and creatively, paint and decorate the house every few years, amongst other things. We expect our fathers to be the main providers for the family, to play with and be loving towards their children, to teach them about respect, morals and virtues, to be intelligent and successful, to be self-made, to run a business, to be caring and sharing with their partners, etc. No wonder most men and women are confused about who they are – let alone what their responsibilities are. No wonder so many thirty-year olds are saying *"Have children? No thank you, I'm just too busy."*

How can we use this?

All children have a mother and a father. This is a symbiotic relationship, the culmination of evolutionary processes on this planet for hundreds of millions of years. In terms of the development of their children, the mother has a more important role in the early years. She breast feeds, she imparts the domestic boundaries and knowledge. However, the father still plays a role in those early years, and he will play an increasingly important role as they grow older. If he didn't have these roles to play, then we would have evolved a different way. Dads stick around, they are programmed to remain on the scene. Unlike other creatures, we are genetically programmed to continue to provide for our youngsters. Out of all the babies born in the natural world, human babies remain with their parents the longest, so a father must have some use.

Just about every book I have ever read on parenting deals with what the mother needs to do. They are almost always written from the mother/female perspective, I'm not being critical, I'm just observing. There is very little literature, information, or advice available for a father who wants to take an active role in his child's development. What information there is tells him how he should copy being a mother. I believe there are separate and important jobs, roles, and tasks a father performs for his children. Instead of these being just a man's way of doing something the mother does, they are actually male ways of doing things, and best performed by men, I call them 'extending the boundary' activities.

Extending the boundaries

I used a lot of examples of the first of these activities in Chapter Two – nature walks, adventures in the wilderness, building camps - being away from home- extending the boundaries of experience beyond the domestic. When men do this they role model the safe extension of the domestic boundaries into new areas in a controlled and loving way. This is hugely important in the development of both girls and boys.

The second group of activities are specifically to do with water – fishing, sailing, canoeing, surfing, etc – all of which seem to be male dominated. As a generalization, men seem to be more comfortable and proficient at such activities than women. Why is that? I don't know, but it is vitally important for the development of our children, they need to feel safe around water.

The third group of activities concerns the taking apart and making of things. Men have a propensity to enjoy dismantling and constructing a huge variety of things – machines, toys, artifacts, houses, etc. Again this is a generalization, but we need to see there are certain things men have a natural tendency towards, which they need to role model to their children and to other children. Men will teach about this activity by just doing it - by being in their shed, workspace, and getting on with it. It is vitally important for both boys and girls to join in, not to be excluded, and they are enabled to see and understand what he is doing. Again these activities relate back to enthusiasm, if the man is enthusiastic about collecting and painting toy soldiers, *(I know, I can't understand why they do this, but lots do!)* let him share this with his children and other children. They will learn a huge amount from sharing the experience, they may not necessarily become model soldier enthusiasts, but something will be imparted about how to be a man, and what it is to be male.

On a much simpler level, a father, or a man, can do a huge number of things with their children in their own way, which will have a lasting impact on them.
They start with:-
* *Holding a baby*
* *The smell and feel of the father is vitally important to babies*
* *Fathers can be rougher and more risk taking in their relationship to their child, they will throw them in the air, they will give them thrills their mothers may be too cautious to provide*
* *A cuddle from your father means something different from your mother*
* *Time with father, play with father, interaction with fathers are intrinsically different*
* *A father tells different stories*
* *A father shows the child different perspectives on the same landscape*
* *A father will invoke a different response within the child when he comes into view*
They develop into:-
* *A father teaches about the outer world, the boundaries beyond the domestic*
* *A father teaches about collaboration, mutual support, how to bond*
* *A father teaches about hunting*
* *A father teaches about sharing and the need to work together*
* *A father teaches about strength and it's relationship to tenderness/boundaries*

32

An example of what a father or positive male role model can do, which mothers tend not to, is shown below.

"Fathers who play-fight with their children are helping them grow into well-adjusted adults. The tendency of men to rough-house and be physical with youngsters has been discouraged since the 1960's, when child psychologists suggested it might be harmful.

Now the first rigorous study of the issue has shown that children with such fathers are amongst the friendliest and most peaceful and popular in the school playground. By contrast, children who are mollycoddled at home and discouraged from rough behaviour are much more likely to turn into bullies or their victims. Charlie Lewis, professor of development psychology at Lancaster University and an authority on child-father relationships, said "There is something special about rough-house play with dads that helps a child to learn self-control."

Such finding will appear counter-intuitive to mothers, many of whom assume that simulated violence and toys such as plastic guns and swords will predispose their children to violence. Such fears are misplaced. Mothers should instead let children and fathers act out their aggression in a friendly and controlled way. It forces a child to confront how he or she relates to other people and it's a safe place to learn rules of engagement."

Michael Durham   Sunday Times, March 2000

CHAPTER SIX
ABSENT FATHERS

The Story

"...Are you all here?" The duck got up and turned around to look at her nest. "Oh no, the biggest egg hasn't hatched yet; and I'm so tired of sitting here! I wonder how long it will take?" she wailed, and sat down again."

"What's new?" asked an old duck who had come visiting.

"One of the eggs is taking so long" complained the mother duck. "It won't crack. But take a look at the others. They are the sweetest little ducklings you have ever seen; and every one of them looks exactly like their father. That scoundrel hasn't come to visit me once."

Interpretation of this part of the story

This is the only reference to the father in the whole story. The absent scoundrel who not only hasn't visited since conception, but also doesn't visit throughout the hard time of bringing up the children. The father who, for whatever reason, is not imparting any knowledge or support to his children, and the most galling part of it is the children all look like him! He obviously was a good-looking fellow because they are all very attractive little ducklings. Unfortunately, this is a very common tale right now.

Resonance for us now

Absent fathers are a rapid-growth industry

Some of them deliberately don't want anything to do with their children
Some of them arrogantly believe they don't have any responsibilities for their children
Some of them don't even know they are fathers
Some of them fight hard and long to gain access to their children, desperately trying to maintain contact

I work in prisons where many fathers pretend to be working abroad, or lose contact because the mothers or extended families feel let down, unhappy, or disapprove. Many keep up the contact initially, but lose contact when they move, when the children grow older, when they have children with other women. Most of these men are still children, they need to be taught how to be fathers, supported in their new role and encouraged to think of themselves as the grown up.

There are so many fathers out there who are not in contact with their children, and the reasons are as varied and as complex as they can be. Children without access to a father are in trouble and need help, but there is no simple answer to this. The Ugly Duckling focuses on the boy's development from a baby through to manhood, and how the lack of a positive male role model affects him. It is a very relevant story for these modern times - *how does a boy grow up with an absent father?* The girls seem to fare better with only a mother. They conform, they adapt, and they flourish. But the boy is unable to conform, he is bullied, unable to fit in, even though he desperately wants to. He is alone in the world, and he suffers hugely for this, he is driven to despair. For me this is crucial to our understanding of the story, and it's relevance to today. When a boy grows up with only a mother, however good that mother is, the boy will always struggle, always

36

feel something is lacking. This is not a criticism of the parenting skills of the mother, it just is a fact. A boy needs positive male role models, and a woman cannot provide them. Without a father he flounders and may be unable to find his place in the world, as we said earlier, even with both a father and mother he may struggle. Even with two of them the child may be neglected, beaten or worse.

We see many cases of parental neglect, they shock the media and press. The wanton abandonment of a young child can seem very alien, and the physical beating or abuse of a child is much more incomprehensible. All of these things are visible, so, it is simple to take a viewpoint and oppose them. However, particularly in the affluent West there are many other ways of neglecting a child, they are subtle and unseen. Indeed, our culture almost encourages them. To neglect a child can be to indulge it. To give a child every material need it requests, but not spend time with it, is to neglect it. We seem to equate good parenting with material provision. This is and never will be a valid way of judging the adequacy of the parenting. Too often we assume just because the child has two parents, both of whom are working and providing material goods, the child should be grateful and content. This is a very contentious area, but there are other ways and means of judging parenting skills and we need to apply these to both mothers and fathers.

Examples from near and far

Throughout the next Chapters I will be discussing the concept of male role models, eldership, and how vital older men are to the development of our young boys. This is not a new concept, but it is important for us to understand how to develop this in today's society, and to use it to alleviate some of today's problems. Many single parent families are incredibly loving, caring and beautiful. I would never wish to be seen to be critical. But, I know boys need a huge number of male role models in their lives in order to grow and become fully mature, self-confident individuals. The same applies for girls. Unfortunately, women cannot provide these for boys, indeed we should not expect women to try to provide them. We need good positive male role models for our children, and, to be honest, a lot of fathers do not know how to provide this, they are still struggling with their own lack of development and insecurities, and often pass them onto their children. In these cases there is a chronic need of a diversity of role models, not just for the children, but also for the father!

How can we use this?
Fathers and Male Role Models
There can be a diversity of different types of male role models and we need to understand their complexity.
The biological father
We all have a biological father, some of us know and love him, some of us are no longer in contact with him, some of us never knew him. He is a huge influence on all aspects of our lives, whether we like it or not. Ideally, we should know and be able to interact with our biological father.

The second father

If not we will have a second father, a stepfather, a man, or a succession of men who take on this role. They can be just as good, bad, or indifferent as the biological one.

The first male role models

Beyond these father figures come those very closely associated male role models who can be very influential. These can be an elder brother, research is only now starting to show how influential elder siblings can be on children. It could be a grandfather, an uncle, a cousin, a nephew, a friend of the family, a father of a friend. The important thing about them is they are real, they interact with the child and can bring a huge amount of good into their lives. They are not the father, they are one step removed.

The second male role models

These can be less immediate, not directly involved. They can be adopted and used by children, especially when they don't have contact with some of the above. Most often they are teachers in the school, leaders in the youth clubs, vicars or priests, any other type of male who becomes significant.

The fantasy male role model

He can be a pop star, a footballer or sportsman, a film/television character, a character in a book, an older boy, someone seen in the street. These tend to be idealized and become distorted in the mind of the child. When the child thinks about them there is a lot of *"If only…"* But, there is an influence here.

The third male role models

When it is time to leave home, a boy will seek male role models beyond the familiar. These should be elders, people who have wisdom, but right now there are very few of those to go around. They should be older by at least 15 to 20 years and act as radio transmitters in terms of where the boy could go. We have neglected this hugely important role, so, many of our teenagers are creating their own role models. Young men are looking for role models two or three years older than themselves. This is where our society fails young men, these slightly older men are not safe role models, they are barely men, and will only teach and preach immature behaviour. Our boys should be seeking older men with wisdom, but where are they?

As a parent you need to look at this list and ensure your sons, and indeed, daughters have a good mix and range of all of these kinds of influences. Talk about them, discuss why they are important, be open about why they are not there.

Pedophilia

Right now our culture has become extremely sensitized to pedophilia, and rightly so. Very few men are pedophiles. This is and always was a minor problem. Somehow, the openness and increased awareness around this issue has been locked into our consciousness with an idealized past. Somewhere in the past, possibly the 1940's and 50's, this wasn't a problem. This is not true. Pedophiles have operated in our culture for a long time. They were more likely to be able to get away with their behaviour then than now. In that sense our culture is actually 'safer'. However, this increased awareness makes all men wary and cautious about helping younger people. That is very sad. I have worked with young people since 1975, such work is wonderfully stimulating, uplifting and challenging. Please do not let others put you off. This work is essential and vital for the long-term survival of human beings. Older men who work with younger men are like beacons of light, they radiate hope and the two attract each other, it is inevitable and cannot be changed.

A boy will be drawn to any number of potential influences. They are all very attractive to him, consciously or unconsciously, he will look to older boys if he has no male role models.

As a parent –
What are you doing about this?
How are you helping him?
How are you making sure that he is choosing those that are going to be the most helpful and benevolent for his development?

If you don't help him, he's going to help himself.

CHAPTER SEVEN
MOTHERLY LOVE

The Story

"Let me look at the egg that won't hatch," demanded the old duck. "I am sure that it's a turkey egg! I was fooled that way once. You can't imagine what it's like.

Turkeys are afraid of the water. I couldn't get them to go into it. I quacked and I nipped them, but nothing helped. Let me see that egg! …Yes, it's a turkey egg. Just let it lie there. You go and teach your young ones how to swim, that's my advice."

"I have sat on it so long that I guess I can sit a little longer, at least until they get the hay in." replied the mother duck.

"Suit yourself." said the older duck, and went on.

At last the big egg cracked too. "Peep … Peep" said the young one, and tumbled out. He was big and very ugly.

The mother duck looked at him. "He's awfully big for his age," she said. "He doesn't look like any of the others. I wonder if he could be a turkey? Well, we shall soon see. Into the water he will go, even if I have to kick him to make him do it."

The next day the weather was gloriously beautiful. The sun shone on the forest of burdock plants. The mother duck took her whole brood to the moat. "Quack … Quack.." she ordered.

One after the other, the little ducklings plunged into the water. For a moment their heads disappeared, but then they popped up again and the little ones floated like so many corks. Their legs knew what to do without being told. All of the new brood swam very nicely, even the ugly one.

"He is no turkey" mumbled the mother. "See how beautifully he uses his legs and how straight he holds his neck. He is my own child and, when you look closely at him, he's quite handsome… Quack! Quack! Follow me and I'll take you to the henyard and introduce you to everyone. But stay close to me, so that no one steps on you, and look out for the cat."

Interpretation of this part of the story

The mother not only perseveres with him, once he is born, she realizes he has things going for him - he's proficient at swimming and quite handsome. Whilst the family is together and not being influenced by outsiders, they are all able to accept him. They give him unconditional love. We all know baby swans are very cute. The perception of him being ugly is only ever linked to the word 'duckling' - he never is ugly. This is so relevant to today's cultural perceptions about beauty and acceptability. We are all born beautiful, we remain beautiful throughout the whole of our lives. No one is ugly. It is only when we are compared to others a perception of inadequacy creeps in, and this is imposed on us by others. Initially our mothers always think we are beautiful, our siblings too, it is only when they meet other people their perception change.

Within the story Andersen uses the mother as the archetype for this unconditional love. Throughout history this has been accepted as such, it is the mother who has the closest contact with the baby and small child, she nurtures him, she holds him for the longest time.

Resonance for us now

Motherly love is also a metaphor, and a very important one. A baby is born with a preconceived view of what to expect, and that is unconditional love. In the womb every need, every movement is accommodated, catered for, the baby expects this to continue. When this isn't true, a baby is in trouble. When a baby awakes and is surrounded by machines and cold hospital walls, s/he is thrown into despair, *where is the human touch, where is the love?* The lack of bodily contact can, and does, deeply traumatize the child. It is not prepared for such coldness, it is prepared only for unconditional love. Such motherly love can be given by the father, by the siblings, by friends and relatives, please don't expect the mother to provide it all. We all have a responsibility when around newborn babies to love them unconditionally, *even though they all look like little turtles or Winston Churchill!* Without this they won't really ever be able to move on confidently into the wider world. They need as much of it as possible - they can't receive too much. This initial acceptance and love gives the baby confidence. The child feels accepted, loved, blessed, and this creates a state of grace within the individual.

"The feeling appropriate to an infant in arms is his feeling of rightness or essential goodness. The only positive identity he can know being the animal he is, is based on the premise that he is right, good and welcome. Without that conviction, a human being of any age is crippled by a lack of confidence, of a full sense of self, of spontaneity, of grace."★2

All of us start out from this place, and for all of us there is a fall from this place. We loose this feeling of 'rightness' and we spend the rest of our lives trying to re-create it. We can spend a lifetime seeking a return to this initial state of grace.

Examples from near and far

Indigenous people, our ancestors, lived in a continuum built around an expectation of this kind of attention. It was closely linked to an acceptance of death and decay as being just as integral to life and love. As we have become more and more civilized we have moved further and further away from these ideas and concepts, until we find it difficult to express love, to talk about our emotions, a very sorry state.

I work with young fathers. A great deal of my time is spent showing them it is good to touch their baby, to hold their baby, to wash their baby, to kiss their baby, to laugh with their baby, to cry with their baby. They desperately want to do all this, but feel inhibited, especially if their baby is a girl. I am sorry, but this is an abjectly miserable state of affairs. We should all be extremely ashamed for having engendered such a terrible way of being in our young people, we all need to work towards changing this.

How can we use this?
On a personal level

We need to understand, maybe we didn't receive too many positive and encouraging remarks from our parents. It wasn't their fault, maybe they didn't receive too many of them as well. The mother says

"See how beautifully he uses his legs and how straight he holds his neck. He is my own child and, when you look closely at him, he's quite handsome..."

This kind of praise is needed in the world. It is the lack of such unconditional praise which has made our present selfish and materialistic culture.   Both men and women can give this kind of support, not only to their own children but to children as a whole. This will have a lasting impact on the way in which we are able to relate to each other and the planet. We must seek to change the way we bring up our children. A vital part of this is the development of unconditional positive regard, as proposed by Carl Rogers. We need to apply it both to our children, *the future*, as well as our parents, *the past*. The more we can come to terms with the inadequacies of our upbringing without apportioning blame, the better chance the next generation has of receiving a good and valuable upbringing.

As parents

We need to accept our children, they are beautiful, there must be an unconditional love for them. This doesn't mean letting them get away with being selfish or cruel, it is not being soft. It means accepting them for who they are. Without this unconditional love the child will always be seeking, they will never really mature into a whole being. When we have been loved unconditionally we can make the transitions from childhood to adulthood more easily and with greater confidence. We can also stand up to the trials and tribulations, the batterings of fate, the bullying, the despair, we are able to take the bad as well as the good.

As mature and whole human beings we need to make sure that every young father we know realizes it is his duty and privilege to show his emotions, to show his child how much he loves, how much he cares, how concerned he is, how afraid he is, and, most of all, how proud he is.

If we are to become elders

An elder has done this work, on a personal level, in a practical way with his own children, and is now sharing it beyond his own immediate family. This unconditional praise is probably one of the most important weapons in an elder's armory of skills and tools. When praise is used correctly and with the right intent it is a hugely powerful tool. When a young man is praised by an elder – it sticks! He remembers it for the rest of his life. This isn't some form of new age wishy-washy *'love everyone and everything'* concept. Praise when given correctly is about the recognition of someone's true value and worth, and giving them a push in the right direction.

Recently, I worked with a group of teenagers out in the woods, camping, exploring, discovering, and being challenged. Many had never been away from home for so long, many had never stayed outside overnight, and the reactions to the stress and strains of such life come very quickly and violently. One particularly troubled youngster was having a really difficult time, he was swearing, kicking, reacting violently to everything...

"It's all crap, everything you're doing is crap, I don't want to be here…"

…and so it went on. As a team we tried to use his anger creatively, without disturbing the whole group experience. We were building a sweat lodge at the time. The boy was taken to one side and helped bow some fire into existence - the rest of us built a wooden structure; covered it with blankets; built a fire; brought several large rocks to red hot; put them into the structure, and doused in water. Sweat lodges are the original form of saunas. Throughout this process, the boy kicked, swore and didn't want to be there. Then came the challenge of sitting in the lodge, knowing it was going to be boiling hot, knowing it was going to be very uncomfortable. He accepted the challenge. In the pitch black, I poured on the water and we all caught our breath as the steam shot up around us. The boy behaved impeccably, helped others, was supportive and encouraging. I noticed this, and as 'father' of the lodge, I remarked upon it, clearly and in-front of the others. He received praise for who he is and what he was capable of, possibly the first time he had ever received such praise. When we had completed the lodge we all stood outside, exhausted, but exhilarated. The boy piped up on his own accord, thanking each one of us in turn for our help, naming specifically how we had helped him, remarking on our own traits in a very astute, humorous, and intelligent fashion. He'd been praised, and now he was showing how he could praise back. He taught me how effective and also inspiring praise can be. For all of us, it was a very moving moment, and his relationship to the other teenagers and the camp as a whole transformed itself.

So, please remember to praise our teenagers, not with blanket praise, but with specific and targeted praise, you never know what effect it may have, not only on the teenager, but on you as well.

CHAPTER EIGHT
SELF CONFIDENCE

The Story

They heard an awful noise when they arrived at the henyard. Two families of ducks had got into a fight over the head of an eel. Neither of them got it, for it was swiped by the cat.

"That is the way of the world," said the mother duck, and licked her bill. She would have liked to have the eel's head herself. "Walk nicely" she admonished them. "And remember to bow to the old duck over there. She has Spanish blood in her veins and is the most aristocratic fowl here. That is why she is so fat and has a red rag tied around one of her legs. That is the highest mark of distinction a duck can be given. It means so much that she will never be done away with; and all the other fowl and the human beings know who she is. Quack! Quack!… Don't walk, waddle like well-brought-up ducklings. Keep your legs far apart, just as your mother and father have always done. Bow your heads and say, Quack!" And that was what the little ducklings did.

Interpretation of this part of the story

In the previous Chapters the story has been idyllic and peaceful. Suddenly, the family is confronted by two fighting families. Welcome to town life, the hustle, the bustle, the arguments, and the proximity of life and death. However, within such a seemingly chaotic scene there is also a clear sense of place and hierarchy. He introduces us to the concepts of lineage, the importance of the red rag, the mark of distinction, which denotes an elder. Such concepts will be discussed in depth later. The elders ensured the young ones remembered their heritage and where they came from. This engendered a feeling of belonging and self-confidence. The lineage and knowledge of our ancestors is even present in the way in which we walk, or waddle! He is showing us the typical life style of the communities in which we all used to live, not so long ago.

Resonance for us now

Up till the early 1700's human beings lived in a way best described as family and village dominated. This is the way we started out many hundreds of thousands of years ago, and is a proven success. The children were the key to the success of a community. On every continent, in every country, the same universal truth applied — look after the children well, because they are the future. One aspect of village life was how cramped, full of people, full of interaction, smoke, smells, fumes, arguments, life and death, it all was. In such communities children became adults through a range of interactions, which to generalize and simplify were along these lines:-

* *At first being held, loved unconditionally, particularly through the female line*
* *As children being allowed to play, run, explore whilst being 'imperceptibly' supervised by parents and the wider community*
* *Being brought up by the whole community, the extended family*

This represented a continuum in the way in which people lived for thousands of years, and only changed radically during the last two hundred years. We have been wrongly taught and continue to believe such life styles were simple and basic. They were not, they were just as sophisticated as our present culture, indeed in many ways they were more complicated.

Examples from near and far

When a child is brought up by the village, or the wider community, s/he receives a diverse, complex and multi-layered education containing a range of influences and guidance, which they can take or leave. Some of the minimum influences of this have to be around the child being praised and nurtured correctly. This doesn't mean we should give our children everything they ask for, but it does mean noticing what a child needs and trying to provide it. If a child isn't given sufficient unconditional love, guidance, support, encouragement, hope, joy, surprises, freedom to express themselves, then they will wither. Some of the most mature and happy children I have worked with have come from the families with the least material goods on this planet. Some of the most self-confident people I have ever encountered had the smallest and most non-weatherproof housing!

A universal comment on indigenous people's lives from all over the world is the lack of parental admonishment or physical violence. to children All intact indigenous people allow their children to have free reign in terms of staying up, running around, playing near fire, etc, etc. This comes from their innate understanding that the children are safe, 'spirit' will hold and protect, as well as the wider community. The complexity of indigenous people's spiritual and social beliefs are impossible to describe here, they are equally complex, and, I believe, more sophisticated to our own. They give a security and self-confidence to the individual and the community we have lost. We are all born with an expectation of this state of being, and it is the lack of this which people bemoan when they say *'where is the community spirit?'* Community spirit is self-confidence.

How can we use this?

We need to examine what self-confidence really is
It is not being arrogant or self-centred
It is not being selfish and ignoring the needs of others

How do we engender it in our children?
By letting them know who their ancestors were
By allowing them to make their own mistakes
By not being overly critical of them
By not being overly protective
By encouraging them to talk to their elders
By listening intently to them
By letting them know we are always there for them
So many different ways

If we are to become elders

We need to know who our ancestors are
We need to be secure about ourselves
We need to have explored our domestic boundaries
We need to have confronted our truths
We need to have learnt from our mistakes
We need to understand that everyone is trying the best they can
We need to be happy in our own skin

We also need to examine why those indigenous people do not physically chastise their children. By doing so they enabled their children to grow up fearlessly. To do so shows a huge amount of belief and strength in the parents and the whole community. In my job I come across so many children who have been shouted at, beaten cruelly, physically tortured on occasions. I know those perpetrators were more than likely treated the same by their parents. The Victorian belief *"spare the rod, spoil the child"* still has an influence in our lives. There never has been, and there never will be, an excuse or reason to physically abuse a child, or indeed anyone. I can remember, as an eight year old, being caned on my hands by the Headteacher at my school. Six on each hand. Then crying uncontrollably as I sat on my hands to relieve the pain. Those who glibly remark *"I was caned and it never did me any harm"* have just suppressed the memory. If we can abolish such actions from our parenting then the future for our children holds a lot less fear, and the violence and anger of the next part of the story can be counteracted from an early age.

CHAPTER NINE
OUTSIDE INFLUENCES

The Story

Other ducks gathered about them and said loudly, "What do we want that gang here for? Aren't there enough of us already? Pooh! Look how ugly one of them is! He's the last straw!" And one of the ducks flew over and bit the ugly duckling on the neck.

"Leave him alone!" shouted the mother. "He hasn't done anyone any harm."

"He's big and he doesn't look like everybody else!" replied the duck who had bitten him. "And that's reason enough to beat him."

Interpretation of this part of the story

When the family steps out into the wider society, they are suddenly confronted by different standards, different agendas. These are created by the village, they come with the society, and when we wish to be accepted into society we have to make compromises. The rule of the mob is a strong and easily manipulated force, which once in motion is very difficult to stop or counteract. The violence was typical for Hans Christian Andersen, he grew up with such brutality, and he writes about it in a negative way. He is writing from his own personal experience.

Resonance for us now

It's such a brutal statement *"..he doesn't look like everybody else...and that's reason enough to beat him."* In the cold light of day it seems so destructive and unnecessarily harsh.....none of us would ever say such a thing, and yet it is so true. We do it subtly, unconsciously, and consciously. We make judgments of others and they judge us. Those judged weird are called by names - *fatty, wierdo, spastic, cripple, ugly*- there are so many different ways of putting someone else down. Whenever you label someone, it is an ugly and de-humanizing process, which can become so cruel and destructive people lose touch with reality and reason. Society creates standards of looks, behaviour and conformity, very few of us are able to transcend these peer-created expectations.

Once we receive our label, what do we do with it? Fight it.....try to change it? *And if it still sticks after many attempts to change it, what is left?* Some of those labeled adopt their label as the truth - if you are told you are stupid enough times, you will believe it. Many children I work with have been told they are trouble and up to no good, eventually they fulfill those prophecies. This process of being perceived as ugly and then adopting the view is very common in today's society. So many young people, teenagers and early twenties have internalized these messages. They create an internal critic expressing these negative views for many of their waking hours, this is directly as a consequence of their lack in sufficient self-confidence to override this criticism. Most have not received sufficient unconditional love so they allow themselves to become deluded. Due to the non-expression of their parents in those initial stages of life, they lack the confidence and self-awareness to be able to see through the label, or defend themselves strongly enough. They accept as truth looking a certain way is better. They will be happier if they are thinner, blonder, wear certain clothes, have more money. So many subtle ways in which we allow ourselves to be influenced and manipulated.

Examples from near and far

Television, Magazines, Newspapers, Advertisements, Hollywood, Peer pressure... it goes on and on.

Fear lurks everywhere, stalks us in our waking hours, seeks our weaknesses and creeps into our conscious thoughts in the most peculiar ways. To stand up against this overwhelming tide is a tough task, but I do believe if you have received unconditional love as a child, and reached some form of completion with those feelings, you stand a chance of seeing the bigger picture in later life.

How can we use this?
On a personal level

When we look at the gangs of kids who inhabit the wastelands of our cities, we fail to see the people. The media likes to ensure we see 'them', not a group of individuals who have names and families. If you are able to gain access to their lives, you will realize they were all born with a name, but in teenagehood, they will often adopt a new name, a nickname. If you are in a dominant position this will more than likely be positive or even aggressive in its nature. However, those on the periphery, those lower down the pecking order, will adopt other less imposing names, and often have derogatory ones. These derogatory names stick, they become an identity, a means of being seen, even if they are bad. Think how desperate a person's life must be to be accepting of a name like *"fatty"* in order to gain some attention, some kudos. The lack of self worth, the lack of self-confidence represented in this act is staggering, and yet a large number of our young people do this.

Recently we ran a weekend for teenagers at which we told the Ugly Duckling story. We enabled them to discuss their nicknames, and all the other tags they had been given. Then through the interpretation of dreams, the observation of nature, internal and external, we came to a new nickname for each of them. One empowering them, one they could be proud of.

If we are to become elders

As I said before we are born beautiful and are diverted from this knowledge by others who pressurize us in subtle and not subtle ways. This conforming and assimilating process continues for many years. For most of us, these are temporary phases we travel through, and the worst damage is the embarrassing photograph to be viewed in later years. But, in the more extreme cases, it can cause a great deal of damage – anorexia, bulimia, depression, suicide even. For many years we will all battle either with the tide or against it. Until one day, maybe when we are 35, or thereabouts, we realize that we are OK just as we are. We look in the mirror and think *"I'm alright with how I look, and I don't care what other people think of me."* This is such a vital stage in life, it is a liberation, a rites of passage of the most important kind. It can only come about through having experiencing depression, anguish, disappointment, all the trials and tribulations the Ugly Duckling will be through. If we assimilate, work with it, we become content with how we look, what work we do, how we dress, and the image we project onto the world. This is the mature realization the desperate attempts to be beautiful of our teenage years are now over. The whole and mature human being welcomes this internal and external change, and now has a life of beauty to look forward to, without stress and worry over how they look or what they do. The immature and underdeveloped human being reaches for the anti-aging cream and phones the plastic surgeon. Our beauty changes as we grow older, we are born beautiful and we are easily loved, we tend to forget this for a number of years, until we re-connect with it through time, experience and forgiveness, and then we truly are stepping into eldership.

Unfortunately, the Ugly Duckling has a long journey to undertake before he manages to transcend the criticism creating his identity.

CHAPTER TEN
HE CAN TAKE CARE OF HIMSELF

The Story

"Very good-looking children you have," remarked the duck with the red rag around one of her legs. *"All of them are beautiful except one. He didn't turn out very well. I wish you could make him over again."*

"That's not possible, Your Grace," answered the mother duck. *"He may not be handsome, but he has a good character and swims as well as the others, if not a little better. Perhaps he will grow handsomer as he grows older and becomes a bit smaller. He was in the egg too long, and that is why he doesn't have the right shape."*

She smoothed his neck for a moment and then added

"Besides, he's a drake: and it doesn't matter so much what he looks like. He is strong and I am sure he will be able to take care of himself."

Interpretation of this part of the story

His mother loves him, she defends him against the most powerful being in the farmyard. The Ugly Duckling has been aware of this and must gain a great deal of strength from her support.

Resonance for us now

When we become parents we become responsible for our children. Part of that responsibility is to create a space in which they can be nurtured, and part is to encourage and support them. In the ideal world we give this support in the form of backing in adversity and unconditional love. The child notices this, becomes accustomed to it, sees it as correct, as his right. He has experienced nothing else, as far as he is concerned this is permanent. This state of support will last forever. These thoughts and beliefs makes him capable of taking abuse and torture, it makes life tolerable despite many adverse conditions.

"He can take care of himself"

This is one of the most important statements in the whole story. I am sure when you first read it, this didn't seem like anything out of the ordinary. You maybe afforded yourself a little chuckle. However, this reaction only reflects how prevalent the view is nowadays. Men and women all subscribe to it, we have all perpetuated it. We moan about men with no feelings, who are aggressive and violent, and yet here is the seed and start of all those behavioural difficulties. Here we have the definition of maleness, it doesn't matter what he looks like, so long as he's strong, and can take care of himself. That is the abridged mother view of what a boy needs to be. It shows how little she knows of what a boy should be, and how essential a father's influence is. The boy needs a far deeper understanding of his maleness in order to become a whole and proper man. He needs to see the subtleties of manliness, the complexity of his father. Without this he is lost. Whilst a mother can support and engender a wide range of developmental programmes within the boy, in the end, he always needs a male role model to learn the essentials of being a man.

"To learn to be the gender you are, you…..need thousands of hours of interaction with older, more - mentally - equipped members of your own gender."★3

Unfortunately, the Ugly Duckling does not receive this, and so he moves towards despair and loneliness. The mothers' motivation is absolutely correct in saying this to her son. It's in her interests to have a tough protector of the family, she has no husband, she wants him to replace the dad. The son took on board the view he is ugly, so, he is bound to believe he needs to be tough to look after himself.

Where is the compassion in this definition of maleness? Where is the ability to cry, to empathize, to be vulnerable, to be joyful, to listen to his heart? If he'd had a father who did these things he would know they were of value. There is the rub - he doesn't have a father - if he had one, *would the father have been mature enough to show his vulnerability?* How many fathers out in the world today have the self-confidence to be caring, sharing and loving in the way the boy needs? Very few. This is the area I work in with new fathers, and it is proving to be very difficult, but rewarding. Some fathers realize they need to be emotional and share their feelings, others still see it as being 'girly', and not manly. The work I do is to redefine the very essence of maleness, and those who see the bigger picture become beautiful role models for their children. One side effect of this work is almost invariably the father develops a better relationship with the mother as well.

The Ugly Ducklings' mother, like so many parents before her, gives him the slightest of nudges, and that tiny nudge hardens his heart, makes him into a tough nut. So many of us have given our children these messages. Our fathers and mothers told us them, just like theirs before. If we stopped for a moment and thought about it, this is wholly not good enough. It is in no way acceptable to expect a boy to be ugly and take care of himself. He is given an identity the mother feels will help him in future life, but it almost kills him. I'm not saying only mothers do this, indeed, immature fathers perpetuate this kind of stuff all the time. *"Don't cry, don't be a baby, men don't do that."* We have adopted a view without question. It is wrong and killing our boys. It leads them to inevitable conclusions about the ways in which they should behave, then we complain when they behave in exactly this way. *When did we start teaching this lesson?* With the industrial revolution, or even before. Maybe when the village became a town. Whenever, it is not needed and is very damaging to all of us. We continue to perpetuate this kind of message as parents, as teachers, and we are surrounded by them in the press and media.

As a pacifist I have strong convictions, I will uphold and defend those beliefs, so, I am not 'girly' or 'unmanly'. As someone who is able to show emotion and be caring, I am not letting down maleness. My children still respect me without my having to resort to violence or intimidation. The teenagers I work with respect me without me having to behave tough or aggressively. I am not a soft touch, but I am also not hardened. When I think of male role models of such behaviour – Mahatma Gandi, Mohammed Ali, Johnny Appleseed, or Henry David Thoreau. They are not wimps, they are not without character, or strength. This passage has really opened up my understanding of how subtle the messages we give our children are. In a sense we don't even notice we have infected our children with a viral disease, it is just a tiny pinprick. However, it festers and is added to over the years by equally insignificant remarks, asides, and jokes even. They all build up, and become a rhythmic way of being, they form the background noise in our busy lives and we adopt them as mantras. Be careful about what you say to your children, it may come true.

Examples from near and far
Example of actively changing the message   1
One of the schools I work in has set up a project for the 10 and 11 year-old children. They are linked to old people in the community. The children enjoy working with these people to create documents about their lives. The adults shared details of their lives with the children that often took the professionals by surprise. Such imaginative projects are a joy to be around in the first place. But one of the side effects from the project was discovered in the subsequent conversations with the boys who took part. They all expressed an interest in the caring professions in the future. They had discovered they were good at being around fragile and vulnerable people. I'm not claiming all of them will now become carers, but I know this is a vital and very important step in the right direction. It is a step towards a more holistic emotional development for those boys, and such a thing is only to be encouraged in my view.

Example of actively changing the message   2
I work on a regular basis with schools in areas of high social need, when I start working in a class I am told certain children are not present because they have been excluded. Almost invariably they are boys. So, I request each one be allowed to come back into school for a day to be my helper. On that day the boy has to be of assistance to me - he has to clean up the mess, he has to help younger children, he has to do as I tell him. They care, they share, and they are seen to be of value. Invariably, those boys behave immaculately with me, they follow me round the school like puppies with their tongues hanging out. At the end of the day the teachers come to me ask about the work.

'It must have terrible having him with you all day'.

I honestly reply *'No, it was a privilege'.*

How can we use this?
As parents
* *Stop and think before you say things to your children*
* *Remember a boy crying is not a bad thing*
* *Remind your boys and girls men can cry, men have feelings, men can be vulnerable*
* *Encourage your boys to share, to be kind, and to think compassionately*

58

As a society

In the Western world there is a chronic gap in educational and social provision, this occurs in the 'caring professions'. With an ever increasingly aged population this is likely to become a crisis of vast proportions, and will inevitably lead to increased social and political unrest. Basically, we have a huge shortage of people wanting to be teachers, nurses, carers – all those jobs essential to the wellbeing of the community. The jobs are essentially about unconditional love, they require the positive regard we spoke about in Chapter Six, and, in an ideal world, they can only be filled by whole and complete human beings – those who have transcended their own personal problems. In order to step beyond our present selfish and materialistic society we are going to have to encourage many more people to take up these professions. At present the vast majority of professionals in the field are female, the percentage of people in these professions who are male is miniscule, below one percent in certain professions.

> *Why has this come about?*
> *Where does it come from?*
> Maybe, traceable to those subtle messages.

CHAPTER ELEVEN
BULLYING

The story

"Well, the others are nice," said the old duck. "Make yourself at home, and if you should find an eel's head, you may bring it to me."

And they were "at home."

The poor little duckling, who had been the last to hatch and was so ugly, was bitten and pushed and made fun of both by the hens and by the other ducks. The turkey cock (who had been born with spurs on, and therefore thought he was an emperor) rustled his feathers as if he were a full-rigged ship under sail, and strutted up to the duckling. He gobbled so loudly at him that his own face got all red.

The poor little duckling did not know where to turn. How he grieved over his ugliness, and how sad he was! The poor creature was mocked and laughed at by the whole henyard.

That was the first day; and each day that followed was worse than the one before. The poor duckling was chased and mistreated by everyone, even his own sisters and brothers, who quacked again and again, "If only the cat would get you, you ugly thing!"

Interpretation of this part of the story

The boy is different, he is picked on for his difference. This is ' at home', the reality for a large number of people, especially in the civilized world! The loneliness which now descends upon his life is shared by millions of people. So many of the people I work with have been bullied, or when challenged admit to having bullied others in their time.

It can and does apply to those of us:-

Whose skin colour is different; who wear glasses; whose clothes are different; who wear different shoes; who have physical abnormalities, be those gross or tiny; who walk differently; who speak differently; who smell differently; whose parents have a different religion; who have acne; who don't have acne; who look nervous; who live in the wrong neighbourhood; the list is endless. The communality holding the list together is simple, the differences are minute. Not one of these differences is actually important.

The Ugly Duckling is abused by his fellow youngsters, this sounds like school to me. School can be a very lonely place for the victim of bullying. Peer pressure is almost invariably associated with bullying and intolerance, because it is the action of immature beings, those who have not learnt or seen how to behave maturely. As we shall see peer pressure will now be exerted on the Ugly Duckling and he will have to resist, and transcend it.

Resonance for us now

I have worked in over 400 schools in the past 25 years, at almost every one of those schools, bullying is a problem. Those who claim it isn't, have either done something about it, or choose to ignore it! We seem to accept bullying as part and parcel of growing up. In certain schools it is almost institutionalized, in many, the teachers are the worst bullies. Linking into the message of the last Chapter, a level of bullying is tolerated, unconsciously and occasionally implicitly encouraged, in most schools. It is deemed to be normal behaviour, and as such a rite of passage. Bullying is not part of a rite of passage, and is not tolerable, whether verbal, physical or psychological. To be bullied is to be diminished, and there is no reasonable excuse for such behaviour.

It is commonly acknowledged that the majority of bullies have been bullied. More than likely in the farmyard there is a duck with a deformed leg, he will almost certainly be leading and orchestrating the bullying of the Ugly Duckling, as he will be relieved of his previous position at the bottom of the pile.

We check our worth and value through the framework of our kudos and standing. This framework is perpetuated by fear, fear of loss of standing, and fear of the unknown, something coming to usurp you. The whole structure is fragile, perpetually in motion, and its balance relies on those tiny differences we mentioned earlier. These subtle nuances of difference mean a huge amount if you want to get on in life. The noticing and conforming to those differences is the starting point of prejudice, intolerance, aggression and bullying. We are immersed in subtle cultural manipulation, by the media, from everyone around us, we don't notice it any more. Bullying and intolerance are the building blocks of war. The tolerance and acceptance of bullying has enabled large amounts of people, countries even, to behave this way. Religious zealots act out of intolerance and attempt to bully others. America acts like a bully. The attempted blackmailing and bullying of Cuba and other South American nations are the acts of a spoilt child. The imposition of your own standards and ways of being are not the actions of a tolerant or mature being. The intolerance of difference is the immature reaction of someone without self-confidence. We need to see the bigger picture. It is essential we oppose such actions vehemently, with courage and strength, not by bullying them back.

Examples from near and far

Those who are bullied can either become bullies themselves, which has no value, or they can attempt to transcend it, this is the difficult path. *How do we transcend bullying?*

For some reason, I think of two films to give as examples here. I watched the 1985 film *"A Class Divided"* and saw something simple and powerful. I would advise everyone to buy this film. It documents the *"Blue Eyes – Brown Eyes"* experiment devised by Jane Elliott in 1968, in honour of Dr. Martin Luther King. I don't want to spoil it for those who haven't seen the film, but I promise it will change your view on school, and how children should be taught forever. Please, please, please support this kind of work. Another moving and very challenging film is the 2006 film *"This is England"* directed by Shane Meadows. Very un-Hollywood, a powerful look at the skinhead culture, and particularly brilliant in it's portrayal of the victims of bullying becoming bullies themselves. It also deals with male emotions, vulnerability and sensibility in a very well observed manner. Such a rare film, portraying multi-layered maleness.

How can we use this?

The bully operates from a position of strength — be that physical, moral or intellectual. However, this is only a perception, and can be changed through opposition. The opposition of the bully is vital to any culture. When bullies are tolerated and encouraged the society stagnates and turns towards dictatorship and fascism. When a society encourages diversity and change it is able to be mature and wholesome. We are a long way from such a place. Often the bully represents the majority view, and as such can be incredibly powerful. William Wilberforce as a social reformer represented a minority view during his lifetime, he opposed the public perception of reality. His perception is now accepted as mainstream, thank goodness. It takes inordinate courage to resist the mainstream, and is the place of the lonely individual. Those who oppose can often find themselves isolated, ostracized, and even more bullied. But fortunately for us, so many individuals and organizations have taken this stance in the past. The opposition of fascism in Europe took a great deal of courage and conviction. The Chartist Movement, The Civil Rights movement, CND, Mahatma Gandi, the Quakers, so many have created precedents and created change. In recent years the women at Greenham Common stood up, and the anti-motorway movement proved you didn't have to be left wing or a socialist to stand up to the bully. The effective way to oppose the bully is to be able to see beyond the popular view, to transcend the accepted norm, and see the bigger picture. As I said, this can isolate you, and the Ugly Duckling is now going to find himself isolated for many years.

CHAPTER TWELVE
PARENTAL BETRAYAL

The Story

   Even his mother said, "I wish you were far away." The other ducks bit him and the hens pecked at him. The little girl who came to feed the fowls kicked him.

   At last the duckling ran away. He flew over the tops of the bushes, frightening all the little birds so that they flew up into the air. "They, too, think I am ugly." Thought the duckling, and closed his eyes - but he kept on running.

Interpretation of this part of the story

The Ugly Duckling is maybe 14 years old. This is the part most parents don't like. It makes us feel uncomfortable and ill at ease. The mother says to the Ugly Duckling *"I wish you were far away."* Until this point he could bear the humiliation and beatings. He tolerated being bullied, and didn't fight back. The withdrawal of his mother's love makes him realize there is nothing holding him in the farmyard and he flies. As far as he is concerned, his mother loved him, and suddenly one day she didn't. This is baffling and devastating. However abrupt this may seem, it is also a natural part of growing up. In a sense, all parents must betray their children, and this happens when the child turns into an adolescent. All parents, hopefully, love and cherish their children, provide a safe environment for them. Then their feelings change. They want this child out of the home- they want the child to leave. One day he was the apple of his parent's eye, the next he's being ushered to the door. From the child's perspective it is a betrayal of all he has experienced so far in his short life. Both mother and father do this, but it can be particularly hard for a boy when it comes from his lone parent mother.

Resonance for us now

"When we are betrayed the toothed side of the universe shows it's mouth: black dogs run behind the carriage, the pitiless cook kills the daughter and buries her in the garden; the misguided groom cuts off the head of the magic horse, and the princess is sent out to take care of the pigs."⋆4

There is no getting away from it, this is a pivotal moment in the Ugly Duckling's brief life. On the surface it is a fearful and fearsome thing. It unleashes untold woes and hardships on the poor unsuspecting youngster. On the surface it looks to be a cruel act. Please don't make too many judgments about this. Understand it is just part of an evolutionary process which has been in existence for millions and millions of years. This isn't just a human phenomenon, it is a regular occurrence in the animal kingdom. The baby lion cub is fed and nurtured, but eventually he is driven from the pride, has to find a territory of his own. Birds bring up their chicks in small nests, as they grow they become too large, they have to quit and fly the nest. It is a dark event, it brings a great deal of despair and grief into the world, but it is also full of potential. Within this moment, many future hopes lie. The parents have to sever the ties binding the child, cut the apron strings. Once they are cut, the parent is only a spectator (at best) in the child's life. But if the parents have done their job correctly the love with which they have nurtured their offspring will see them through to maturity.

Examples from near and far

The transition which is adolescence can be little more than an act of faith from the parents perspective. They have done their best, they have loved and supported the child, now it is up to the adolescent to run with it. There is an element of risk here. There is a real risk that the boy will fail, make a fool of himself, get hurt, die even. But, he can't stay where he is, he will become fat, idle, lazy, an irritant, we don't want that. So, change must enter our lives.

The way in which we have constructed our society means a lot of us are afraid of change, when we feel this way, we seek to construct very immobile and solid structures. We attempt to insulate ourselves, our homes, our children. By doing so, we don't allow in the cold North wind. This may seem sensible, but it isn't. It is a short-term measure, and inevitably the North wind will come, and our children will feel it. When they feel it, they will be afraid, but it will also attract them. It will change everything, whether we like it or not. Without change we stagnate. Change is adolescence and teenagehood Welcome to the cruel world little Ugly Duckling. He has chosen to leave the farmyard, make a new start, turn his back on both the love of his mother, and the cruelty of the other animals. His decision is a clean break and he moves quickly into a new world. A strange and unfamiliar place, and yet he still carries the stigma of his previous life. Even at the moment of departure he says *"They, too, think I am ugly."* He has been defined, defined by his mother, by his family, by the farmyard for so long he has now internalized the message…I am an Ugly Duckling. He carries this with him into the world. It is his life's mission to battle and overcome such a cruel hindrance.

How can we use this?
As parents

This is a tough stage of life for the parents. As a parent, you force/allow your offspring out into the world. There are many things we could do at this point in life, here are just a few. We need to recognize it is just a part of an evolutionary process, there is no guilt attached. We need ritual at this moment in time, for the parents and for the teenager. There is no alternative, and the lack of ritual at this time and throughout our lives brings us closer to extinction as a species by the day. I make no apology for speaking this way, I know this to be true, I know it in the core of my bones. If you can't get your head round this then we are all lost.

As Malidoma Somé says *"Where ritual is absent, the young ones are restless or violent, there are no real elders, and the grown-ups are bewildered. The future is dim."*★5

There is a great deal of grief attached to this separation, and grief is very healthy. In order to work with the grief you might seek to create a ritual. It might include some of the following:-

• The parents need to talk to people they know have been through this stage of life. The parents need to acknowledge their pain and shame - tell of the grief, cry, let out all the deep-rooted pain, and this can be unexpectedly difficult. Especially if they haven't been initiated themselves.
• When working with grief I have often placed a large rock crystal in the centre of this work, as a focus and container for the grief. The parents need to be encouraged to direct their grief into the stone, whose nature is to receive, and which forms a real and solid core to the process. We need to offload safely, and without judgment. If the grieving is to be achieved without judgment it needs to be in the company of elders

who know what you are experiencing. Someone who hasn't been through this stage of life will not be able to hold the grief as well. This grief is also an accumulation, it goes beyond just us. It has been passed down the line by generations not being able to keep a clean bill of emotions- who didn't do this work.

•   This grief turns naturally to praise once it has been dealt with, and the parents are able to praise and honour their children as part of the ritual. This is very important, as we need to be able to rise above the grief, see where it is leading us. It leads us to growth, and an ability to bless others, without being held back by inhibitions and pent up emotions.   If the parents have grieved enough, they are ready to release their children into their independent lives.

They need to bless their children on their journey, and this can take many shapes and forms, here are some suggestions:-

*   *Unconditional love - honouring the child, blessing their nature without condition or prejudice.*

*   *Hearing their dreams - allowing them to state their vision, not judging it, then honouring and blessing it.*

*   *Holding them - either physically if requested, or just in the space, to enable the child to know s/he has been held. This can be for a long time!*

*   *Blessing their journey - giving them a little physical/symbolic bundle of wisdom and food for the journey, reminding them that they take a part of their father and mother with them, wherever they are.*

*   *This can be a very moving and cathartic experience for all involved, and it is a huge blessing on those participating, those watching and holding the space.*

I have been privileged to participate in such work, I know what this is about, and the amount of tears to be shed is immense, please don't be put off by that. We organised a retrospective ritual for men and women who wanted the opportunity to experience this kind of ceremony. It was incredibly moving, deeply transformative, and enabled people to bless their own parents even if they were dead or no longer in their lives.

If we are to become elders

The departure of a child from the home can be a very prolonged and torturous process, especially when we don't have any rites of passage or rituals in our lives.   In a culture where the extended family is the norm, they would give the father and the son an intermediary, someone who wasn't directly involved, an uncle or similar person, an elder. He would be able to listen to the teenager and to the father. He could give a different perspective to both, take the heat out of their exchanges. He would remind the father of his own wild times, encourage the teenager to take responsibility for his actions. Laugh at their serious and earnest troubles, encourage them to see it as just a phase they were both going through. No need for psychological counseling, no need for suppressed anger, no need to tear each other apart. We have lost such a complex understanding of community, how multi-layered and interwoven it is, our communities are very thin in comparison.

Our dysfunctionality as a society comes from our inability to see the importance of support, the importance of listening and just spending time with each other. Parents need to spend time with their teenagers, it will help everyone.

CHAPTER THIRTEEN
THE ASCENT

The Story

     Finally he came to a great swamp where wild ducks lived; and here he stayed for the night, for he was too tired to go any farther.

Interpretation of this part of the story

In the context of the Ugly Duckling being about rites of passage for a teenager this represents the first stage of the rite of passage, ascent. He will now rapidly fly away from his home, driven by rage and despair.

I was on the earth, I walked this life, I know who you are and how you are
I was a baby, a child and then a teenager
When I was a teenager, I rejected my society, I rebelled
I was wild, I went insane, I needed to do this
I rejected their company
I went to live in the wilderness
I contemplated wildness, I felt hurt
In that state I was in pain
I knew my wounds and I saw their worth and value
By accepting pain I was able to transform it into love
I transformed my pain into love by understanding how to go with the flow
By crossing the threshold
I went deep into the earth, with my pain, not leaving it on the surface
The pain came with me, and by going deep into the earth I was able to cross into another state
A state of grace, acceptance and serenity
All men need to do this, they need to plunge into the earth, wholeheartedly, and accept the consequences of their actions
Then come back to become of value to their society

Grandfather Pipe Carrier

In simple terms the story starts with the main character being in a state of grace, he is born perfect. Through no fault of his own he is then persecuted, he is able to bear the torment because of the love of his mother. When she betrays him, he is in pain, he flees the home. He carries the pain with him. He flies upwards and away. This is the start of an ascent, an ascent away from the home, from all he has known into the unknown. It is fuelled by his disappointment, his despair, his anger. He flies out into the world at a huge velocity. This is vitally important. The speed generated will carry him into the wider world. It is a very positive thing. Ascent away from the home creates new horizons, new experiences, which are of importance and significance. All boys need to be in ascent, however, as with all ascents there will be a descent. In our culture we have a huge number of men in ascent, being propelled at a velocity they can barely contain. Because they are not initiated, because they aren't held in a safe space, because they don't know about boundaries, they become addicted to ascent. If we had been through a rite of passage we would have been held by older men, and we would have been warned of the dangers in ascent.

Resonance for us now

An essential role for the father is the creation of safe boundaries. The competent father will not only create these safe boundaries for his children, he will be consistent in their application. The creation of consistent and well-defined boundaries imparts a huge amount of security to the children, and it encourages exploration. When we have safe boundaries we feel safe to explore, we know we are held. A father does this for his children, and particularly for the boys, this is a vital lesson. When a boy spends time with his father and amongst older men, he is being given these consistent messages, and he absorbs them. He recognized them within his own DNA, he respects them intuitively, they are teachings about becoming a man. The mother cannot do the same job. I know this statement will upset mothers, but I know it to be true. Imagine the other way around, and the father is expected to give advice and assistance to his young teenage daughter about menstruation. It would not work. In general terms, the boundaries defined by the mother apply to the domestic, the boundaries defined by the father apply to the wider world. This reflects the inter-related nature of the female and the male. The complimentary skills which the two possess. When combined they create the whole. When one aspect is missing, the message is incomplete. If the boy doesn't know where the boundaries are, he flies beyond them, out into a very different world.

This is very common nowadays. There are hundreds of thousands of young boys without viable male role models, who are presently beyond boundaries. However hard their mothers try to give them boundaries, they are broken, ignored, and unnoticed. So many of the families I work with have this problem. The boys show little respect for the mother's boundaries. They leave home without the ability to reign themselves in. They leave feeling let down, in pain, betrayed, they therefore create a tough shell, a hard outer coating with which they confront the world. This crystallizes and forms into a belief - *'no-one can tell me what to do with my life'*- it often manifests itself as a lack of respect. A lack of respect for boundaries and the law - which he would have received from his caring father - if he'd had one.

The Ugly Duckling is out in the flat lands and this marks his ascent into loneliness, he has traveled beyond the known territories and he must now become familiar with the totally unfamiliar. The special loneliness the boy now encounters, is a male phenomenon. He is separate and alone in the world, in a way a woman or girl never can be. He has not been shown what it is to be a man, he doesn't know where he is going, but he is still undertaking the journey, in a sense, he is forced to. He is forced by the cruelty of the other farmyard animals, by his own complicity in the lie about his ugliness. He believes he is ugly, this belief manifests itself as a pain, it is a cut, metaphorically speaking. He is perpetuating a lie, and when he does this there will always be something missing in his life. Deep within his soul he knows he's not ugly, he knows he's a swan. If he had been given that knowledge, if elder men had supported him, his experience of the world would have been very different, possibly not so lonely, possibly not so fearful, certainly with more self assurance.

His soul, his innate nature, is the part pushing him on. Even though it is not conscious, it is now taking over. He is on a quest, a quest to find the truth about himself, in an attempt to come to terms with his pain. The only place he can find this is outside the home. If he stays in the farmyard he would only ever be the Ugly Duckling. By being alone and seeing what he is capable of, without his mother's support or love, he may find his souls' purpose. He may die as well. These are desperate times, and they call for desperate measures. It is an ascent at a huge velocity, it will either make or break him. There has to be the possibility of death in this ascent, otherwise it will not be real.

I know in our homogenized culture this seems very brutal, but it is the truth. The Ugly Duckling is a pre-industrial revolution story, it deals with the essential nature of the world, and in it there is the potential for great love and joy, as well the potential for harm and death. We try to protect ourselves from the 'hardships of life' - by centrally heating our homes, by not mentioning death, by always being with other people, so many different ways. But, in the end, these are false luxuries. We fail to do ourselves justice as human beings by softening the corners of our reality. In the end we become soft, malleable, conformists, who have forgotten how to love, how to scream, how to enjoy life. We believe we have eradicated fear from our lives, yet we have actually increased and engendered it thousand-fold. This story is about the real world, a world full of love, compassion, hardship and despair. The story is about accepting fate, welcoming change and diversity, which doesn't conform to the familiar. We've forgotten such a life used to be normal, and was accepted as such for thousands of years. This kind of lifestyle still exists, just outside our window frames, just on the edges of our perceptions, and it will continue, long after capitalism and materialism have disappeared.

His mother says *"Besides, he's a drake; and it doesn't matter so much what he looks like."* She defined him, the female aspect of life, his own internal female, and he is unaware of the other side of himself- his compassion and his humility. He battled against the image, but eventually he buys into it, he internalized the message. When we also remember the second part of that message *"He is strong and I am sure he will be able to take care of himself."* We can see how he is now alone. He was defined as ugly and able to look after himself, no wonder, he is now fulfilling that prophecy. So many of the teenage boys I work with believe themselves to be hard, to be alone, to be untouchable by emotions. So many of those boys have been given that image by their parents. This self-image will be a tough and difficult burden to bear. I'm not being critical of the mother, she did the best job she could, she imparted the knowledge she knew about. But, it was incomplete.

The Ugly Duckling has fled the nest as a half-baked beast, not fully ripe, nor fully formed. His chances of survival in the bigger world are much less than someone who had a competent and loving father. That loving father or positive male role model would have shown him it is acceptable to feel emotions, to be vulnerable, not be too hard. As a culture we need to examine why we believe men should not cry, and to see the long term damage this is causing within our society, not only amongst men, but amongst women as well. The effect on a daughter of seeing her father cry is huge, and we need to come to terms with how important this is. Both boys and girls need to see men who are vulnerable and able to grieve. Men need to cry because of the cruelty and beauty of the world, it is not a sign of weakness, it is not unhealthy or unwelcome, it is a very natural reaction to the world.

Examples from near and far

Daedalus in his escape from the Labyrinth with Icarus constructed wings and flew to safety. He built the wings from feathers and wax, and before the two set off he warned Icarus not to let his wings touch the waves and get wet, and not to fly too high as the sun would melt the wax. But the young Icarus, overwhelmed by the thrill of flying, did not heed his father's warning, and flew too close to the sun, the wax in his wings melted and he fell into the sea.

Like Icarus most men are so enamored with their wings and the rush of ascent they pay little heed to the perils of descent. I know many men in their fifties who are still in ascent, I am still there myself. We need to know about descent, but like the Ugly Duckling and Icarus most of us don't have mentors to show us the way down. If we had received good guidance, we'd have been taught about the true nature of our souls' purpose and as a consequence our falls wouldn't be so precipitous. But, for now lets look at what ascent means for boys. Up until this point the end of the world was the Minister's wheat field. Already it feels as though he has gone beyond these. The immense pressure of despair and depression has propelled him beyond the known world. He is catapulted beyond safety, and as he never received the message about boundaries, he is now through them.

How can we use this?

I recently worked with a group of young fathers in the Rhondda valley. A historically tough area. Associated with the coal and steel industries, with men who lived and worked close to death. These young fathers are the first generation without a coal industry to go into. They strike me as being people who have spent a long time in a very dark place, they are emerging blinking in a bright light with hands outstretched not sure where they are going. They are trying to learn skills and techniques their fathers and grandfathers didn't have and couldn't pass on. They have to be kind and compassionate to their partners, form relationships with women based on mutual respect. Many are now prime carers for their children, because a lot of the jobs available in the area are for women. It is a very scary and difficult transition they are making.

The culture into which they have been born held up a certain macho way of being as the male ideal. This was perpetuated by their parents, and to a certain degree by their peers and partners. Many of these men, starved of the opportunity to go down the pits, leapt into a very rapid ascent fuelled by alcohol and drugs abuse, inevitably leading to incarceration and hardships. They found their hardness inside prison, they returned to what they thought was acceptable and ideal, through their crimes and anti-social behaviour. In amongst these patterns of behaviour many became fathers. For some of them becoming a father was the pivotal moment in ascent. They found themselves in fatherhood. Suddenly, they had a purpose and a belief in their ability to be a father. Not all of them did, but for some of them it happened. We are now working with these fathers to tell their stories, to create their myths and archetypes through their diverse experiences. We will be telling those stories to younger boys and girls in schools. Using the experience and knowledge these dads have accumulated to pass on a very special message. Boys can care, boys do love, boys are capable of being emotional without losing dignity and respect. I know the men will be honest, sincere and concerned, something those children will remember for a long time.

In the 1990's an Elementary School in New York undertook an experiment, which became hugely successful. They were a failing school, and the academic achievement level of the boys was well below the girls. They advertised a volunteer scheme asking for men to come and work for a few hours as teachers support staff in their classrooms. Many of those who volunteered were professionals, and their task was to do as the teacher (all women) told them - so they tidied up mess and spillage, helped younger children, and generally did as they were told. They became male role models for the boys, who saw men listening to, and obeying, women. This was a revelation for many of the boys. They hadn't seen this happening at home, or in their neighbourhoods. Over a period of years the academic achievement level of the boys rose and stabilized. The project cost no money, it didn't take huge amount of the men's time, it didn't impact hugely on the school, didn't undermine the authority of the women teachers. This is how simple the work is, but it also reflects just how vital important it is.

These examples show the diversity of people who can be positive male role models. These men could have criminal records, they can be teetering on the edge of a return to addiction, they may have been through humiliation, they can be lawyers and pillars of society. So long as they are trying to make a difference, trying to be honest and sharing. Often when we think about positive male role models we connect back to our own preconceived ideals, and we need to be careful about that. Too many parents and teachers think you must be squeaky clean, they have preconceived ideas about who could qualify for this role.

Maybe they want an academic - someone who only talks about it, but doesn't actually live it. Maybe they want a man who can be easily dominated by women - someone who is weak and soft, who has no backbone. Maybe they think of the false idols of Hollywood, the hollow and superficial image focused on celebrity not depth. All these can perform the role, but they can also be terribly boring and dull.

Often they are not what they seem. They can be wonderful, or they could be still fixed in an immature behavioural pattern they can transfer to your child. I'm not saying all male role models need to have criminal records that would be very foolish and naive of me. Male role models are as diverse as human beings can be. All I am saying is please don't pre-judge men who on the surface may seem to not be ideal. A role model can be those people who have had tough lives, but are now vulnerable - are now able to see compassion and forgiveness. These can be magnificent men who deserve to be supported, deserve to be given acclaim. I also know to become a good male role model, you need support, you need training, you need to be given time to develop your identity. It is not simple, and yet of course, for some of us, it is easy.

CHAPTER FOURTEEN
BRAVES

The Story

In the morning he was discovered by the wild ducks. They looked at him and one of them asked, "What kind of bird are you?"

The ugly duckling bowed in all directions, for he was trying to be as polite as he knew how.

"You are ugly," said the wild ducks, "but that is no concern of ours, as long as you don't try to marry into our family."

The poor duckling wasn't thinking of marriage. All he wanted was to be allowed to swim among the reeds and drink a little water when he was thirsty.

Interpretation of this part of the story

He has ascended and suddenly he finds himself amongst his peers. He is now at the beginning of the second stage of his rites of passage, peer initiation. Here he meets similar aged youngsters. He bows to them, he wants to become friends, and they in turn are interested in him. He starts to become familiar with boys of his own age who are in similar circumstances.

He's not thinking of marriage, so this gives us a good idea of how old he is, and what he is about. He is old enough to leave home, but not old enough to be making a home of his own. In all indigenous peoples this stage is called warriorhood. To be a warrior you need to be between childhood and adulthood. The state of warriorhood can be a variety of things, it lasts many years or not, depending on the tribe you belong to, and your personality. Unfortunately, I know what I mean when I say warrior, but many people don't. The word incorporates 'war' and the whole concept around indigenous warriors has nothing to do with war. So, in order not to be misunderstood I will use the word 'brave'. This is the name some of the Native American peoples gave their young teenage boys, and it is such a beautiful word. To be a brave you don't have to be strong, you can be vulnerable when you are a brave. I much prefer it, it has a multiplicity of meanings, all of which are useful in this context.

Resonance for us now

To be a brave is a natural stage in any boy's development. It can not be avoided, there is no way of becoming a grown up, without going through this. In the limited time I have spent with indigenous peoples, I have been able to glimpse the truth of braves. There are two parts to being a brave:-

The first is the freedom to express yourself, to create who you are

The second is to know that you have responsibilities to others

These are not mutually exclusive, if undertaken in a well maintained rites of passage.

A brave needs to have certain freedoms, certain allowances made for him, he should not be confined or restricted. The freedom is given because it is understood this is only a phase he is going through, it is not permanent. He needs to be as free as he can, he needs to be wild, in order to eventually return and become an upstanding and useful member of the community. If he is not given this freedom, he will not be liberated, he will remain stuck. He will continually be in the state of mind with which he left home - confused by his parent's betrayal, alternately wanting to break the ties and wanting to be mothered. He will be stuck in ascent as we are in the West.

The brave needs to be able to create his own identity. He needs to break the ties with his family. His mother can't do this, even his father can't. It needs to be done by people who are outside his immediate nuclear family. He is ascending away from his parents so the last people to be able to do this work are his mum and dad. He needs bridges being built to safely guide him away from the home. This is logical and absolutely common sense, and yet, how do we support this in our culture? We expect the parents to do the work without assistance, no wonder our young men are so confused. The brave is no longer restricted by his home life, but that mere act of separation doesn't define him. The brave needs to go through a process of liberating himself, in order to find himself. He is in the throes of individuation, the creation of his identity, the new man.

Only by being free to ascend can he really explore and create his personality fully. All indigenous people understood this, and were able to be flexible enough to have this process happen within the structure of their society. Ascent was part of the culture, it was understood to be very necessary. They didn't turn their backs, they welcomed it in, they knew it was vital for the perpetuation of their culture. We aren't free enough, secure enough, in our societies' well being. We frown upon the 'inappropriate' behaviour of our teenagers. We make them into outlaws, people who live outside our cultural setting. They do their teenagehood in the lowlands beyond our fields. The Ugly Duckling undergoes his brave training and initiation outside society. That is an extremely dangerous way of growing up.

Examples from near and far

The braves of the Lakota tribes of the Americas were the ones who killed the buffalo for the families and individuals in their tribe who couldn't hunt. Their responsibility was to become so good at hunting buffalo they could provide for the others who couldn't provide for themselves. In return they were able to lead very independent lives, without responsibilities, and without family ties.

The L'murrani (braves) of the Samburu tribe in Kenya are able live very freely, they spend a huge amount of time painting and adorning themselves, but are fearsomely protective of their tribal lands. To our outsiders view they may look like dilettantes and posers, but they are being supervised in their teenagehood by the elders. They are given the responsibility of looking after the cattle, these are vital and essential to the wellbeing of the community. They represent the wealth of the community. Each family has goats and sheep which they take care of themselves, but the L'Murrani look after everyone's cattle as a whole. They will be punished severely if they loose cattle. They will kill those who seek to steal the cattle, they know the dire consequences to the whole community if the cattle are lost. They are given clear boundaries even within their freedom.

When a boy becomes a brave they are expected to eat and drink with their fellow initiates, indeed, no brave is allowed to eat or drink alone. They must collaborate with each other, this has been a major feature of all teenage rites of passage. The apprenticeships undertaken in the steel industry taught all jobs were dangerous, you needed to be supported and work as a team. The coal industry was the same, when you go down a pit, you can't do the work on your own, you must collaborate, you must work in a team. This showed the boys how to ask for help, how to share, how not be hard, but how to be softened.

Reciprocity

We are by nature hunters and gatherers, it is commonly accepted wisdom the men were primarily the hunters, and the women did most of the gathering. Both activities are collaborative, both activities depend on co-ordination, the sharing of knowledge and support. Certain aspects can be undertaken by an individual, but for the greater part, they are activities which need many hands. It is in our nature to assist each other, and this is within the male gene just as much as within the female gene. As fathers we need to keep this very much in mind, indeed, it is our duty to impart this to our children, and most especially to our boys. Hunters did favours for each other, they helped each other with specific tasks, and asked for those favours to be returned. To catch large animals is a collaborative process, so when one family wanted to catch a large animal it sought the help of others outside the family. When successful, the meat was shared, but there was a debt accrued. When the other family wanted to do something else, the original family collaborated and re-paid their debt. The mutual indebtedness of the families created communities. That is the basis of all communities, the give and take. This leads us to reciprocity, the push me pull you, of evolution. The older men's role is to show the boy about reciprocity - if you give you will receive, if you share others will share with you, if you ask for help, it will come. Many of the social problems of today's disillusioned youth boil down to this point. Teenagers haven't been shown how to share. They are surrounded by selfish role models, mostly perpetuated by the media and the press.

In addition, they haven't learnt about the importance of their elders, they haven't been shown respect. Almost every day in the media we have people complaining about the lack of respect shown by young people. Respect is reciprocal- if you respect someone they will respect you. You don't receive respect just because you reach a certain age. That isn't how it works. If you don't respect young people, they won't respect you. As the more mature partner in the relationship it is down to the older people to show the younger ones how to do this. Older people need to show respect before they will be respected.

How can we use this?

On a personal level

This is rather a large subject, really it should be dealt with in another book, but I want to just touch upon a few concepts. Reciprocity applies to all things, our relationship to each other, and most importantly, our relationship to the planet. We need to see beyond our present culture – it is not founded on reciprocity and therefore, I think most people will agree, fatally flawed. We need to understand the world doesn't depend on oil, material goods, or capitalism to exist. It is now commonly accepted only by mutually assisting each other and other species will human beings continue to live on this planet. There is an urgent need for a world-wide re-education programme.

As parents

We need to think creatively about how we want the next generations to be brought up. We need to learn from the past and create a more holistic future. This all comes down to good parenting, which is personal, individual, and impossible to define. However, one of the many principles of good parenting has to be the teaching of reciprocity. We can teach it in many subtle ways. Almost invariably pocket money involves reciprocity, or, at least, it should. If you do your chores you will receive some money. If children have been shown this, their ability to go out into the world and make something of themselves is increased. If the child has never experienced this, the outside world can become a very fearful place, and may intimidate and confuse the child.

If we are to become elders

We need to be able to step beyond the ordinary, we need to see beyond the confines of our present culture and be brave. We need to challenge the norm, the way of the West, and we need to trust that something new can and will be created. When we become elders we use our unconditional positive regard to transcend the accepted views and to create an unknown and unforeseen future. One where war and violence have been eradicated for instance. That would enable us all to move towards reciprocity through redemption.

This may seem rather grand and presumptuous for a little book on ducklings, and, as I said before, it is a huge subject, but I believe the message needs to be here. Elders need to work towards a future in which there is not a need for war, for violence, where hunger and destitution are actually combated, and where we all support and encourage each other. If men learn to see it as part of their job as human beings to become part of that movement then we really know something is changing. Without vision and hope what is the future?

CHAPTER FIFTEEN
PEER RITES OF PASSAGE

The Story

He spent two days in the swamp; then two wild geese came - or rather, two wild ganders, for they were males. They had been hatched not long ago; therefore they were both frank and bold.

"Listen, comrade," they said. "You are so ugly that we like you. Do you want to migrate with us? Not far from here there is a marsh where some beautiful wild geese live. They are all lovely maidens, and you are so ugly that you may seek your fortune among them. Come along."

Interpretation of this part of the story

This sounds like an offer of peer rites of passage to me, and like all young men, he goes with the flow, *wouldn't you?* He must accept the offers coming his way. The Ugly Duckling has no alternative, so he goes for it, he lets go of everything he has known, and accepts what comes his way.

> *'There is a river flowing now very fast. It is so great and swift that there are those who will be afraid. They will try to hold onto the shore. They will feel they are being torn apart and they will suffer greatly. Know the river has its destination. The elders say we must let go of the shore, and push off and into the river, keep our eyes open, and our head above the water. See who is in there with you and Celebrate.'*

The Elders, Hopi Nation, Oraibi, Arizona

He is out in the river, those of us who cling to the shores will be torn apart and suffer. It is an invitation to walk on the wild side. When we ignore the call of the wild we remain domesticated. We become the thirty-year old men who still live with their mothers. The scared and frightened nerds who prefer the company of cyberspace women to the real thing. We all have to jump in, and trust that some day we will surface and be able to keep our heads above water. This is not just a message for teenagers.

As a species we are in crisis, the planet is in crisis, it is time to let go, there is no alternative. The human race is at the teenage stage of development - it is behaving badly, taking drugs, and staying out late. Human beings have the opportunity to grow up, become proper citizens of the planet. We need to go through a species-wide rites of passage, *and who is going to hold us through that?* Now there's a thought.

Resonance for us now

Young men are being forced to initiate themselves into manhood because we've given them no other choice. We are not offering any alternatives. As with Chapter Ten we are back in the territory of peer pressure, and with this comes compunction, force, bullying, coercion and many other subtle and not so subtle pressures. When we are unsupervised in the creation of our rites of passage, they will only ever perpetuate myths:-

From the teenage perspective

*   *The myth about old people not understanding them*
*   *How only teenagers know what they are going through*
*   *You are a man if you take drugs, drink alcohol, drive fast cars, play with guns, treat women badly, pick fights, etc.*

From the elders perspective

*   *The myth about teenagers being sullen, idle and work-shy*
*   *Teenagers are not like they used to be*
*   *Because the older people feel a lack of respect they complain about how things used to be better, even though they were probably a lot worse!*

Examples from near and far
Different rites for different people

There was a planet-wide acceptance of the importance of rites of passage for young people, to celebrate their journey into adulthood. This is an ancient tradition it has been in existence for thousands of years. The last vestiges of such traditions are still to be seen all round the world, although most of them have lost their original connections and meanings, they are still adhered to as being significant and important.

A rite of passage ritual should reflect the society in which it is undertaken. The Samburu, a nomadic warrior tribe, need to know that their young men will defend their cattle and lands with bravery, so they circumcise the boys. A settled agricultural culture doesn't need the same from their boys. In the West we are so confused about who we are, and what our culture is, we have lost all contact with the concept of rites of passage anyway. Whether this is a good or bad thing is up for debate, all I know is we are complaining about lawless and aggressive teenagers. One way of reintegrating and encouraging these teenagers would be to reintroduce the concept of community led rites of passage. That doesn't mean we should introduce the un-anaesthetized circumcision of our young men, there is no need, but there is a principle which could be applied. Indeed we have a fantastic opportunity to be able to create new and different rites reflecting who we are presently are, and encouraging space for individual expression and compassion.

How can we use this?

We need to set in motion the creation and development of new, modern, rites of passage for teenagers. Few of today's young people recognize they need a rite of passage, let alone actually want to endure the hardships of such rituals. And yet they are doing this work already. Our boys are initiating each other through the tribal patterns they create for themselves. At present, we are allowing them to do this, and they can devise any number of challenges for each other, including:-

   *   *How much alcohol you can consume, every year many young men die from alcohol poisoning due to binge drinking.*
   *   *What drugs you can take, leading to addictions, criminal activities to support habits, vandalism and anti-social behaviour '.*
   *   *Having fights, picking fights with total strangers in the streets or clubs, again this can often lead to hospitalization and, on occasions, death.*
   *   *Driving cars whilst under the influence of drugs or alcohol, again leading to damage of property, hospitalization, and occasional deaths.*
   *   *The rape and gang banging of girls, leading to physical abuse and damage, psychological trauma and long lasting damage, again creating huge social problems.*
   *   *Tattooing and body piercing, the creation of identity, this can be done with dirty needles, without proper equipment, leading to hospitalization, permanent scarring and poisoning.*

These are just some of the ways in which our young boys are presently becoming men. The actual cost to our society of these actions in terms of lives, time, money and grief is immense. As a society we have chosen to allow them these options, rather than the safety of a rite of passage under the supervision of older men. The cost of such neglect is in millions and millions of pounds and swamps the National Health Service and other agencies. The net benefits to our society if we were to take community led rites of passage seriously would be the equivalent and more of the present costs of unsupervised peer initiation – it would make economic sense to reintroduce community held rites of passage, let alone spiritual, ecological and planetary!

CHAPTER SIXTEEN
BLOOD

The Story

    "Bang! Bang!" Two shots were heard and both the ganders fell down dead among the reeds, and the water turned red from their blood.

    "Bang! Bang!" Again came the sound of shots, and a flock of wild geese flew up.

    The whole swamp was surrounded by hunters; from every direction came the awful noise. Some of the hunters had hidden behind bushes or among the reeds but others, screened from sight by the leaves, sat on the long, low branches of the trees that stretched out over the swamp. The blue smoke from the guns lay like a fog over the water and among the trees. Dogs came splashing through the marsh, and they bent and broke the reeds.

The poor little duckling was terrified. He was about to tuck his head under his wing, in order to hide, when he saw a big dog peering at him through the reeds. The dog's tongue hung out of its mouth and its eyes glistened evilly. It bared its teeth. Splash! It turned away without touching the duckling.

"Oh, thank God!" he sighed. "I am so ugly that even the dog doesn't want to bite me."

The little duckling lay as still as he could while the shots whistled through the reeds. Not until the middle of the afternoon did the shooting stop; but the poor little duckling was still so frightened that he waited several hours longer before taking his head out from under his wing.

Interpretation of this part of the story

This is the third stage of the rite of passage. He has taken part in peer initiation, without supervision, and it has ended in blood. The failure of peer rites is important as it creates boundaries. He sees death and only just escapes, he must be in shock and severely shaken by the experience, he will now be a little more cautious about life. The failure of peer rites leads to wounds and the opening of wounds, these can seem very damaging to us, but they are actually beneficial.

I live on the air
The air supports me in my flight
I adjust my feathers, minutely, with care
When I want to take off
I have to open my chest
I have to open my chest to spread my wings
When I do this all my wounds are rent open
All the wounds in my body expand
In that expansion
The internal light shines through the wounds
The light within is allowed out
Only by opening my chest can it shine
By doing so, I show who I really am
My true identity is revealed
My wounds proclaim my beauty
My wounds, my hurt, my sorrow, shine out as I fly
They illuminate the world as I fly above it
I claim my place in the universe by being open-chested
By risking to show my wounds in their true light
Grandfather Buzzard

We are now entering autumn, there is a chill in the air, we are no longer in the warmth of summer. The ganders and the Ugly Duckling try to initiate themselves, in the end, this leads to death. A rite of passage is by its' nature linked to death. When you move from being a child to being an adult, there is a death, you are no longer a child. A rite of passage is the opening of a door to another world, often it is hard, and frequently this may be a close encounter with death. Many people who have had a close encounter with death say *'it changed my attitude to life'*. Such experiences make you think, not of death, but of life, the rest of your life - and what are you going to do about it. We all need to be sharply reminded of our mortality, because especially as teenagers, we can often think we are pretty invincible. The Ugly Duckling left home with the pain of his disappointment from his mothers' betrayal, he carried it with him as a metaphysical cut, and now he comes across the physical manifestation of this pain. He has to open up his chest and feel the pain.

Resonance for us now

Blood can be a huge part of rites of passage for boys. Women come naturally to such a time in their lives. The shedding of blood for boys seemed to be an important part of almost every rite of passage in indigenous peoples all around the world. Rites of passage are about blood brotherhood, the shedding of blood, and by shedding it, a genuine and honest commitment to being in community. This is the reality, it is not sanitized, nor is it something we deal with every day- this is special and difficult.

The rite of passage for a brave, particularly those still living nomadic existences, has a huge amount of pain in it- it can come in the form of circumcision, scarification, tattooing, many different ways. The brave welcomes pain. He moves towards it slowly, reluctantly, but irreversibly. When he encounters pain, he holds it within himself, and then he transcends it. He steps through pain and into an enlightened, spiritual, place. When he does this as part of his initiation he does it on a number of levels. He does it out of respect for his past, his ancestors; he does it under instruction from his elders who have also submitted to this process; and he does it with his peers who are supporting him in the process. The physical pain of initiation, is expected, it makes sense. Once it has been transcended the benefits for the individual and the community are immense. As a man he gains respect and trust from those around him. He is able to call upon the recollection of the ritual pain in later difficult situations. He can use the memory to gain strength and courage. He gains self worth and assurance, it increases his self-confidence. The benefits to the wider community are equally significant. An initiated boy is far less likely to bully others, is far more likely to help others, he is prepared to collaborate and mutually support others. The boys who pass through the ritual will form strong and life long bonds of friendship. They create strong communities. Such men are more likely to be content, not restless, and less likely to break the law, in a sense they carry the law in their bodies.

These rituals stimulate bravery. Bravery comes as a surprise in our culture, in indigenous cultures bravery is expected and encouraged. How many stories do we have of individuals finding unexpected strength in adversity, such memorable transformative experiences. These are part and parcel of a warrior tradition. When they are part of your culture, part of your existence, they become day-to-day occurrences. The inter-relationship of pain, bravery, and respect needs to be examined without our blinkered cultural expectations. In ritual the pain transcends the personal, the pain is shared within the family, with the wider community, and by our ancestors. We don't have such rituals, and we have a very confused relationship with pain. Almost all of us are scared of it, we take it personally.

*"If nothing else, it begins as an awareness of the fear itself. And then, somehow, you pass right through fear, right through the pain. You enter a realm both within and beyond fear and pain. So long as you feel pain, it means you're thinking of yourself. Only when you stop thinking of yourself can you actually get past that pain and that fear. You've got to forget yourself to find yourself. You yourself are the entry way."*6

Once you have been through such a process you can come to terms with those things worth being afraid of, and those you can't do anything about. As a culture we spend a lot of our time worrying and being afraid of unimportant things, of things we can do nothing about. That is the behaviour of an uninitiated person.

Examples from near and far

We may well feel that such blood rituals are cruel and brutal, indeed they are. I have participated in a circumcision ritual for about a hundred boys between the ages of 9 and 19. It was the most brutal and scary event of my life. When we only connect with the act we don't appreciate the social significance, the importance of sacrifice. We are surrounded by sacrifice, but we have spent a lot of time and effort in disguising and covering it up. For example the animals we eat all sacrifice their lives for us. The Samburu honour this by eating and using every part of the animal, down to drinking the blood of the goat. They specially slit the throat skin to retain a flap onto which they can carefully run the blood so it can all be drunk. This is a highly respectful act, in no way gross or barbaric. Being barbaric is to breed and raise animals in confined spaces, pump their bodies with drugs, throw away most of the carcasses, and pretend you don't know about it.

A Samburu boy sacrifices himself in the ritual. He is circumcised as a gift to his ancestry, as a gift to the elders, and to the wider community. By being circumcised they are committing themselves to stay within their community. They are showing how much respect they have for their ancestors and traditions, and accepting the laws and rules of their tribe. The circumcision is a symbolic acceptance of their responsibilities to the future as well. They are showing how seriously they take the coming responsibility of parenthood and guardianship of their tribes land. They are prepared to go through such a depth of pain without flinching, without movement, without anesthetic. The pain is transcended because of the support and acceptance of its significance.

It would be impossible to replicate such a barbaric act in our western culture. Indeed it would be wholly inappropriate. We do not live a nomadic existence, we have no real sense of community or family. It would be very useful to develop our own equivalents,

92

and to explore ways of creating and managing them. Unfortunately, at present, the depth of commitment to community is not present in our teenagers. Crucially, it is not present in our elders, so they would not be able to 'hold' such a ritual. The Samburu ritual I participated in took place in 2006, it only occurs every fifteen or twenty years, so it is very doubtful that it will ever happen again. It was one of the last vestiges of an expression of community commitment which we all possessed tens of thousands of years ago. It is a physical embodiment of a spiritual connection as ancient as we are. Hans Christian Andersen recognized this in his story, the shedding of blood, and the facing of pain are vital elements of the whole.

How can we use this?

When we do this work it is beyond the confines of Health and Safety. That is what makes such work worthwhile and precious. However, it also makes it very difficult to gain funding or receive backing from local authorities and charitable trusts. In one ceremony I organized the men involved decided that they needed to wrestle. Normally we have a contract at the beginning of work, and this states 'no violence'. We created a circle, held it with some rhythmical drumming, we agreed that anyone who stepped into the space was no longer held to the contract. It represented a huge challenge to these men who had led pretty safe and protected lives, many of whom had never been involved in a fight before. One by one we stepped inside. After several hours, two broken ribs, and many bruises, we finished. This happened years before the book and film *"Fight Club"*, but like them showed how relevant and important danger and physical challenge is to work with men. Without an element of challenge, fear, and the potential of failure, a rite of passage really isn't true. A lot of our teenagers are doing this work already, and a lot of them are hurt and killed because they are unsupervised. It is time we did something about this, and replaced it with supervised challenges and rites. They will take a lot of preparation and training to create and maintain, something for the future, but we should be working towards these goals. We must be offering our young people a more viable alternative. There are many ways in which this work can develop and flourish. The seeds of such work are presently being sown – nurture them.

Example 1

I ran a weekend vision quest ceremony for young teenage boys. During this we took them out of their city environments and put them into nature. It would take too long to describe everything here, but they experienced some challenges. Being woken at 5.30am in November, being sent out into the dark wilderness as the snow fell! They survived, we worked intensely with them around the concepts of mystery, the unknown, the magical. As teenagers they struggled with these concepts, their astutely developed left sided logical brains fought us every step of the way.

We weren't making much progress, one evening I said

"Tonight you are going to dream, when you wake up, I want you to write the dream down immediately."

They dreamed and wrote them down. We asked them to describe their dreams.

One had dreamed he was in a fairground, and was asked by people he was familiar with, but didn't know, to try out the attractions. As he went from ride to ride he continued to meet friendly people he recognized and yet didn't know. Finally, he had tried and mastered every ride, and was given a t-shirt from his favourite band as reward.

I was so pleased, I asked.

"So what does this dream mean?"

He spent a little time thinking, then replied.

"I like fairgrounds?" I almost pulled my hair out at that moment.

We worked with another person's dream, and suddenly we could see the boy was starting to understand the symbolic nature of the experiences. We went back over his dream, he explained it beautifully, and very poetically. He felt it represented his experience with us.

Finally, he said.

"And now I realize that I knew those people, because they were aspects of myself, they were parts of me."

He had cracked it.

Example 2

At the end of a ceremony the adult participants were blessed by a young teenage boy and girl who hadn't participated. The boy spoke of his thanks for the elders of his tribe being prepared to do ceremony on his behalf. He was a particularly vulnerable and yet toughened boy, with a very troubled background. As the ceremony broke up I realized the men involved needed to honour him, so we took him off to a dark place. I wanted to honour the way in which he had been able to talk in front of such a large crowd.

From somewhere in my heart came an urge, and I tend to go with such things. I jumped on him, held him down to the ground, he fought me, I pressed down on him, and a very angry, scared look came across his face. The other men followed my lead, we pinned him to the floor in dark silence. My face was pressed tight against his, looking hard into his eyes.

I said quietly and with authority.

"I see you, I know you, I know what you did... "

He squirmed with fear and apprehension, used to being admonished.

"...I saw you being brave, I love you for being such a brave young man, I love you for being such a good talker in front of so many people...."

On I went.

His face relaxed, his breathing eased off, he smiled, and started to laugh. The rhythm of his laughing body was connected to all of ours, we all melted into a laughing heap in the dark. We then showed him a 'grief bundle' we had wrapped in cloth, and explained how we had grieved the bundle into existence. For us the bundle represented abuse, shame and corruption of power, and our wish to stop such things. We didn't want to pass them on to the next generation. We had undertaken the work so that he didn't have to carry the bundle. It was a very emotional moment for us all. He helped us bind the bundle up. We said we trusted him, we gave the bundle to him, and asked that he bury it for us. No one went with him, it was a commission of trust. He was very proud about being given such an important task. These stages of the ceremony were completely unplanned, yet complemented all which had gone before, it was very moving and beautiful. If we hadn't seized the opportunity he would not have been honoured. He will remember it for a very long time.

If we are to become elders

The ganders and The Ugly Duckling are fired upon by guns, does this sound familiar? The shedding of young men's blood has been part and parcel of our lives for a long time, although we are presently trying to ignore it. The two World Wars and subsequent ones have been drenched in the blood of our young people. We feel squeamish about putting young men through a rite of passage in which they are tattooed or undertake some kind of ritual cutting, but we have no compunction about letting hundreds of thousands of young men die on our behalf on foreign soils. As a society we need to examine how and why we are allowing our young people to experience such trauma. We seem content to ignore the consequences of such acts and expect our young men to return from the experience without assistance and help. The example of American service men in Vietnam and subsequent outbreaks of Gulf War syndrome and post traumatic stress disorders in service men all over the world highlight how dangerous unsupervised and unsupported rites of passage are. These men need counseling, support, honouring, recognition, and celebration. They need the whole community to recognize the kind of sacrifice they have made on our behalf, and receive support from elder men who have been through similar experiences. Most tellingly they need to be able to grieve the things they have seen and the inhumanity of their experience, we have neglected their needs. As a society we have to recognize it is our responsibility to ensure such neglect is not repeated, not swept under the carpet.

CHAPTER SEVENTEEN
RUNNING AGAINST THE WIND

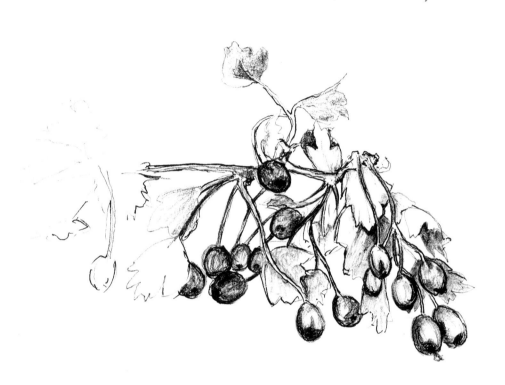

The Story

Then he ran as quickly as he could out of the swamp. Across the fields and meadows he went, but a wind had come up and he found it hard to make his way against it.

Interpretation of this part of the story

The Ugly Duckling is now on the run, fighting against the wind. This is the fourth stage of rite of passage, the introduction of caution, after the adventure of peer initiation. Here he is alone and by being alone, he can spend time contemplating who he really is. Away from the influences of the farmyard (his family) and the other young men.

Resonance for us now

Rites of passage are gateways from one way of being into another, and one of the reasons for doing it is to recognize who you truly are. The last event, and the next few, are very traumatic and will change the Ugly Duckling's life. By living through these events he will mature, leading him to a new awareness of who he is, and what he is capable of. The testing of his mettle will reveal his true self.

He still thinks he is ugly. He doesn't need this any more, but he is still carrying the baggage. Remember in the last Chapter. *"Oh, thank God!"* he sighed. *"I am so ugly that even the dog doesn't want to bite me."* This isn't true. The dog ignored him because he stayed still and he didn't panic. Only when he has developed sufficient self-confidence will he recognize himself, and often this is achieved after an older man has helped. This used to happen with apprenticeships, the boys went into industry and tried a range of skills, they were given groundings in all areas of the business. They were given these by specialists - older men who had particular skills. These older men then selected the boys they felt most suited to their specialization. They recognized a particular talent or leaning within the younger one. The boy's selection meant he had a long and hard training in a particular area, this could take years. It was not in the older man's interest to have boys who didn't want to do the work with him. The decision was made on ability, the latent talent within the boy, which these older men were able to see.

Examples from near and far
Rites of passage from around the world

Before the male initiation ceremonies of the Tzutujil Mayan Indians of Guatamala started, the old men sat outside the compounds of the potential initiates and waited for him. The mother, aware of them, stood defiantly across the doorway, shouting-*her son was nowhere near ready to become a man, he was still just a child,* and for the men not to take him. They didn't. They sat and waited. The boy was inside the compound listening to his mothers' wailing lies and cries. Eventually, it was his decision to come out, it was his decision to go to the older men. He told his mother so, and the ties were broken by him, not her. She had performed her part of the ritual, as had her son, he'd started the initiation process.

In Bali the predominantly Hindu community participate in a ceremony called "Matatah" which pre-dates Hinduism. This is the practice of filing the front six teeth on the upper jaw. It is seen as a means of passing into adulthood, the girls do it after their first menstruation, every child participates for a two-day period in the ritual. The reasoning behind the ritual is the dulling of the canine teeth, which will make the individual calmer. These teeth represent the "Sad Ripu" – the six enemies of the human soul – lust, greed, anger, drunkenness, confusion and jealousy. The ceremony is undertaken by the older men of the community.

The Bar Mitzvah for boys and Bat Mitzvah for girls of the Jewish religion are undertaken on reaching the age of 13. This is a relatively new tradition, it is not mentioned in the Talmud, and the elaborate ceremonies associated with it are a very recent phenomenon. In it's simplest and earliest manifestation the celebrant is asked to recite a blessing over the reading from the Torah on the Saturday after his birthday. Nowadays, as the ritual has become more complex, the celebrant is required to learn the entire 'haftarah' including its' traditional chant. He then makes a speech beginning with the words *Today I am a man…",* followed by his father giving a blessing for being no longer responsible for his son's sins. After which they have an elaborate celebration. The ritual is evolving and becoming more complex which seems strange in this age of forgetfulness. Again it is the boy becoming a man and proclaiming such in front of the elders of his community, those who help him to learn the text and chant.

In Central America there is still knowledge of past rites of passage celebrations for the boys. The practice has died out due to the incursions of our perverted 'civilization', but a memory remains. They tell of a year-long ritual which enabled the young boys to learnt the 'male' language, having previously spent most of their time amongst the women and only learnt their language. Being based in a pastoral and fishing culture the need for extreme rites like the Samburu, was not there, but the ritual was still a hugely difficult and strenuous time for the young men. The boys were mentored and cared for by older men during the whole year, and they impart a huge amount of knowledge, language and many other things in their time together. The rite represented a test on all levels, not just physical, but also spiritual, and in terms of his ability to connect to the mystical, the unknown, the unseen. However, there was also a huge amount of compassion in the rites of passage, the mentors were able to show their empathy and love. The whole community took part and supported the work, and it had a deep influence on the every day lives of the community. Again, it was organized by the elders and the privilege of such work was understood and taken very seriously.

In my heart I know these faint glimpses of the deep past are the real thing, they are authentic, they touch upon a principle, the root of all rites of passage for young men. There are many, many more examples. We should not try to re-create these, we should try to create new ones, relevant to today, but most especially relevant to our young people's needs.

How can we use this?

"Rites…together with the mythologies that support them, constitutes the second womb, the matrix of the postnatal gestation of the placental Homo sapiens."[7]

Rites of passage are essential to the growth of an individual, they are unavoidable, and a very necessary part of our maturation, however, we cannot force people into them.

A boy must want to do it. He must come to this conclusion and ask older men to help him to pass through it. If this element isn't present then the rites of passage can be shallow and not of such great value, especially, if it is done for him. It must come from within. On the morning my son, age 16, went to have a sweat lodge with older men to welcome him into the start of adulthood, of his own accord, he went in and woke his mother. Kissing her on the cheek he said

"That's the last time I kiss you as a boy."

You can imagine how much his mother cried. When we sat in the silence and dark of the lodge that afternoon, a unprompted small confident voice stated

"Thank you men for coming here today, you are all the bridge over which I will walk to my manhood."

You can imagine how much we all cried that day! But we all acknowledged his wisdom and character.

This defines rites of passage, the recognition of who you are by your elders. Rites of passage are hard, they are simple, they do not offer a simple option, indeed, they must be tough. By being so difficult they enable the individual to find the right path, if they were over quickly then the path may not be the right one. If it's too simple he will probably choose the path suggested to him by others - by his parents, peers, or school teachers - in this case, the path of the Ugly Duckling. Parents, peers and schoolteachers can't do this work. These people will impose previously held views, or influence the individual. This work must be done by elders, who have the interests of the individual at heart, also the interest of the wider community. Their interest is to see the individual recognize who he is, by doing this he will return to his community, and contribute fully. If he doesn't do this properly he will always be doubtful, and that is no good for the community, you can't rely on someone who doubts himself.

"Rites of passage then, are community-centred. Benefit accrues to the community. Of course, there is added benefit to the 'client' who has, via her existential passage, resolved the problem."[8]

The Samburu understand this principle and they have incorporated it into their rites of passage for the braves. After circumcision the young men are trained for fifteen years, they are able to paint and decorate themselves, they use red ochre to paint and adorn their bodies, particularly their faces, they use beads to decorate and thread their hair.

They are given the freedom to express themselves fully in this. Each warrior may take hours each day decorating and cultivating a particular look for himself. Through doing this he eventually creates a unique image. This includes what he wears, how he stands, where he stands, it is all about attitude and style. The elders know each brave must do this, in order to 'get it out of his system'. Once they have expressed themselves in this way they start wanting to settle down and to have a family, as each generation, or age set, has done for hundreds of years. The Samburu named their present youngest age set L'Kishami, 'the beloved', the generation before them were the L'Murli, 'the unopposed'. Each generation is named every fifteen years or so, because that is how long it takes the boys to become men, even though they experience the circumcision ritual in the first year. Through this long period of ascent they create themselves, they express themselves fully, without restriction, and then they come down into descent, and are happy to settle down. Again the brave comes to this decision by himself, he isn't forced to it – 'your six months are up, go get a job'. That isn't the way of the Samburu or any indigenous people.

The individual must have fought and battled to find the true path, and in a sense he must have despaired of ever finding it, he must have stepped right into the darkest parts of himself in order to find the true nature of his soul. It's not enough to do this work with only part of your mind or soul. This is wholehearted work, full of despair, failure, achievement, disappointment, desire, pride, ownership and eventual success. When completed there is such a deep sense of success, pride and accomplishment. It is about self-confidence and pride. The individual needs to be proud of himself, to see his wider community is proud of him, and so he takes pride in his community. This is a simple process, yet the effects of it are incredibly powerful.

The minimum structure and framework for such work are:-
- There must be elders, guardians, who know what is possible, who have been through the process themselves, who guide the initiate.
- The initiate needs to want to do this work, he must be mature enough to understand this work is needed.
- The initiate must be challenged, must be pushed beyond his normal experience and boundaries.
- He must learn that he needs the help of others, he must learn about reciprocity.
- He then needs to be alone, truly alone to confront his darkest aspects, and to find his souls' purpose.
- When he returns from this lone vigil, he must be acknowledged, praised and welcomed as a new person, transformed, not the person who started the rite.

THE MISSING CHAPTER
THE ELDERS

The story

The Ugly Duckling continues outwards and alone, because that was the way Hans Christian Andersen experienced it. However, I am sure he also knew one of the things lacking in his life were elders. So, let's talk a little about them, before we return to the story.

Resonance for us now

Over the last 30 or so years I have specialized in working with teenage boys, and am acknowledged as an expert in this field. During this same period it has become increasingly obvious that we have a major problem with these people. I hope these two facts are not related!

I work with government departments, local authorities, charitable trusts, and they all ask me the same question.
"What should we do with young people?"
My answer is almost invariably baffling.
"Release the elders from their enclaves."
In order for our boys to pass through being teenagers and to become men, we need elders who are interested enough, and feel committed sufficiently to take this work seriously. Our teenagers need a good range of role models and midwives to help them through the troubled times. By doing this work we create wholesome and vibrant communities. However, these elders have to know what is suitable and useful for these teenagers, how to initiate them, and what rules to lay down.

Who is doing this with today's youth?
Social workers? Teachers? Youth workers? etc.
Do they really know how to do this work?
Or are they only being used as nannies or policemen and women?
They are employed by us to 'take care' of young people, so their main concern will always be for the society, not the young people.

How can a youth worker offer the kinds of rites of passage these young people desperately need, when s/he hasn't been initiated? The great majority of youth and community workers are in their 20s and 30s, and to be honest they are not elders, many are not old enough to do this work properly. They are not the right type of role model, they are unable to impart the depth and breath necessary for teenagers. I know it may sound as though I am being dismissive of youth and community workers, I am not, I am just saying young ones are not necessarily good ones. What I am saying is teenagers, need and are drawn to older people, it is seen in almost every household, the connection between the grandfather and the grandchild is very powerful and useful.

Children's Home model

I was employed to work in a children's home in Germany for three years in my early twenties. I had been involved in some pretty dark dealings, and I actually had a lot in common with these young people. The children's home I worked in was run on 'family-like' principles. There were three groups of children, each had a full time male and female worker who took responsibility for the overall group. These workers were supported by us - the full time and part time assistants, work experience students, and volunteers. This was a very effective way of educating and re-integrating these vulnerable and damaged children. The older men and women were the children's and my role models, my elders. The ways in which they taught me about life were simple, but extremely powerful. The men taught me by just being themselves, by just being lovely older men. I remember one evening I spent with Claus, a man in his forties…..I thought he was so old. He invited me back to his house for a meal and to meet his family. My memory, which is still so strong, is the two of us listening to Neil Diamond records, him smoking a pipe, and his budgerigar singing in the background. Despite the fact that I had previously thought Neil Diamond really old and rubbish, I started to listen to the words of the songs, and was moved deeply. I remember both of us sitting with tears rolling down our cheeks, crying at the depth and beauty of the words and sentiments. I enjoyed that evening so much. It showed me what life could be about in so many ways- I will always remember it.

The bonds formed by all of us through our mutual experiences were incredibly strong, and they have stood the test of time. This summer I was visited by one of the 'children', she is now 45, she and her three children stayed with me, and I am still in contact with my male role models. They were true elders, those children are well on their way to becoming elders as well, and I learnt a huge amount from all of them.

Examples from near and far
Elder training
To initiate young men into adulthood we need older men. Right now we have an aging population so we have a huge resource available for this job. We are not using them at all, in this context, or in so many other ways. The majority of older people are living in ghettos, cast out from society either voluntarily or involuntarily, and consequently they are feeling rather bitter and depressed right now. Many of them would be ideal for the job, but a large percentage would need training before I would let them loose with teenagers. Mainly because they have learnt to be bitter and scornful, this is not useful or conducive to unconditional positive regard. So, the rather longer answer to those questions I am continually being asked, is put teenagers through community led rites of passage, run by appropriate elders, who have been trained. Without the appropriate elders in place any rites of passage will be flimsy and worthless. So, the first step must be towards retrospective rites of passage for elders, you can't put a teenager through something you haven't experienced yourself. These elders need to be in their 40s and 50s, and need to be able to see the value and worth of such work. Form an orderly queue here please.

Earlier I wrote about the difference between a warrior and brave, and I realize our teenagers don't know the difference either. They are peer initiating each other into becoming 'warriors', if they had elders to guide them, they would be helped to become 'braves'- that makes me feel so sad. The lack of male role models means we are perpetuating a myth, and it is a real matter of urgency to create a new way of being. First of all, we need to recognize an elder when we see one.

Elders

Elders are the ones who can make light of the darkest situations, because they have been there themselves. They are the ones who have the depth of experience to knock the cockiness out of these brash teenagers. They are not like the boy's father, they are of the grandfather's age. The importance of this age difference has been known about since time immemorial.

I used to work with an ex-sailor and soldier, Jack Sullivan, who passed away a few years ago, blessed be his memory. He used to come with me to some of the very troubled schools I worked in, and would sit at the back watching proceedings, most of the time I would struggle to remain in control. He would just observe and help the children to draw, as he loved drawing. In one troubled classroom he stepped forward and accosted one of the teenagers who was particularly aggressive.

"So, you're a gangster are you?" Jack asked.

"Yeah, I'm scary, dangerous and hard." Came the glib reply.

"Have you ever killed anyone?" Jack asked with a wry smile on his face.

"Well.......no...but, you know." Came the slightly deflated reply.

"I have." Said Jack quietly.

At the end of the lesson this untouchable, hardened boy was literally sitting on Jack's lap, he had regressed to being a six-year old, if he'd been able to suck his thumb he would have.

"Please, Jack, tell me another story."

Jack had tamed a complete tear-away in less than an hour, I couldn't do it, I was just in my 30's and I still haven't killed anyone!

I frequently took older men into the schools with me. I took a group of retired coal miners into a school in Nantyglo, up the South Wales Valleys. They sat conspiratorially in the back row of the class as I worked on an environmental project. At the end of the lesson the teenage boys came up to me, one said

"Those old boys were disgusting."

A genuine look of bewilderment on his face.

"They know all about SEX." He gasped. He'd never thought older people would be like that.

Older men can do a job the mother, the father, and women can't do. They can confront teenagers with the truth. They know what the teenagers are going through, they can support them in creative and imaginative ways. Ways the parents can't even conceive of! But, they must be full of life, mischief, and adventure - not moaning old farts sitting at home complaining about the world. The older men need to know what it is to have lived and to encourage their young charges to be adventurous too.

An elder is an older man who has let a lot of things go. For me a father needs to accrue and accumulate material, physical and practical things, in order to provide for his family. This is a very necessary phase in life and will teach us a great deal. However, it is not linked in any way to becoming an elder. An elder has been through this stage, and is in the process of letting it go. He doesn't want the clutter and accumulation of his previous life, he is simplifying. This simplification process is the next phase of human evolution, summed up in that wonderful phrase *"You can't take it with you."* Just as the initiate boy walks towards pain, the necessary pain of initiation into manhood, an elder walks towards death. The inevitable ending of his days which we all have coming. When he walks towards it willingly he is free, liberated from the every day concerns, previously so important. He is able to be as childish as he likes, or as serious, it doesn't matter.

A boy becoming a man is an initiate, and a man becoming an elder is an initiate too. All initiates accept the pain of initiation as a gift to their ancestors, and it is their hope that it will liberate them into the next phase of life. We used to be well versed in the inevitability of our life and death, and cognizant of the ways to pass between the ages of our existence. We seem to have lost the memory of this, temporarily, I hope, and we seem afraid to grow up or to change. It is inevitable, a boy wants to become a teenager, he accepted the pain of initiation as something to be tolerated before he can become a man. It is inevitable that your children will leave home, and you will not need to have the same physical or material goods. We are all moving in the same direction and you cannot stand still or turn back time. When we resist and try to fight against this, we create fear, illness, pain, and stress. If we fear the inevitable we extend our inability to accept our fate, by remaining uninitiated, immature and without hope, we create more fear. A true elder has been initiated into manhood and initiated into eldership, and in the end he will be initiated into death. In the West we cling to life, our old people have their lives extended into pain, inaction, fear, despair, loneliness, confusion and anger. This isn't eldership. It's an uninitiated extension of childhood, promoted by fear.

An elder needs to breath death and life. He needs to be at ease with sacrifice, and the passing of the seasons. He needs to know about all of this, and to have experienced it all many times, he needs to have fought against it, overcome his fears, sometimes, and other times not. Such an individual is not afraid of teenagers, he is not afraid of anyone! If he hasn't started to learn these lessons then he can't teach the younger generations, he will be too similar to them. He will have no wisdom to impart, he will only pass on knowledge, not wisdom. Many older people have experienced a great deal and made a 'success' of their lives. That is fine, but it doesn't mean they can inevitably teach others. To teach others you have to have processed life, processed it internally. Asked hard questions of yourself, as the Ugly Duckling has done. Most importantly, been able to find and face the answers, however tough they might be. The distillation of knowledge into wisdom is not simple. Wisdom needs to be imparted in very specific ways. Without attachment, with as little ego as possible. Encouraging personal exploration, supporting individual growth, not through dependency or reliance on the teacher. We need to also accept the inevitable consequence of evolution is the next generation will learn more than us. But on the way they may well make mistakes, which could have been avoided. Such is life.

How can we use this?

Like the Ugly Duckling many teenagers are now being initiated into manhood by their peers, and many don't have a clue what they are doing. I think that is OK, it's not great, but at least the work is still being done. We are trying the best we can, and our teenagers are trying desperately to make sense of their lives and our culture. I know they will become beautiful and whole human beings at the end of these processes, it just may take a long time.

If you are a parent or someone in your thirties or older, then I would implore you to think about the fact this is called the missing chapter. True elders, as described here, are missing right now, not just here, but throughout the world.

Maybe it is time to do something about that
Maybe it is time to start giving back to our communities by working without fear alongside teenagers
Maybe it is time to retrospectively put yourself through a rite of passage
Maybe it is time to acknowledge how you have already done this work, and to recognize how balanced and at peace you already are

If we are to become elders

We need to acknowledge what we have learnt, how we have learnt it, maybe unconsciously, and to then offer it to others. I work with an organization called the Circle of Life Rediscovery, and they organize and facilitate outdoor camping experiences for teenagers. I work for them because I know what I am doing, I have worked with teenagers since 1975, and they recognize having a strong and personally confident male as part of their team is vital. Through the years of facilitating this work with them they have employed, and had as volunteers, many people. It is always fascinating to see how suitable, adaptable, and capable these 'older people' are. Many have never worked with teenagers before, and see it as something easily achievable. Because teenagers are so sharp and extreme, almost inevitably these 'elders' start having to deal with their own past and really struggling, they are confronted by their past, not something they expected. Ally this to the conditions of working in a forest, under canvas sometimes in the continual pouring rain for many days. Many self-assured and confident 'elders' leave as timid wrecks and never come back again. This never happens to the teenagers! Indeed it is the opposite. *Why does this happen?*

These individuals, however old and experienced they may be, have not consciously been through the processes of rites of passage themselves. They may have a lot of experience, just like the Ugly Duckling will over the next Chapters, but it was never formally structured or led by elders. These individuals are attracted to the work because they need the work for themselves. Unfortunately, we are not facilitating the process for them- it is for the teenagers. Many come and want to join in the sweat lodge or other activities being offered, and we have to gently dissuade them. They need to do the work themselves, before they can be of help to teenagers. Once again, training for elders is needed so badly and by so many.

An elder facilitates an experience for others, and receives the rewards in a variety of subtle ways. The rewards are in the witnessing of moments of revelation for the teenagers, and that is sufficient. The teenagers either get it or don't, and you can never tell beforehand when the lesson will be learnt or what the lesson will be. The elder doesn't take the process personally, doesn't say *"I made that happen"*, this would spoil the moment, and cheat the teenager of the experience.

An elder doesn't have to force or bully a teenager into an experience. A true elder is so attractive and interesting to teenagers, and to the rest of his community, he develops respect and trust instantly in those around him. He doesn't have to operate in the ways which younger people do. I try to teach this behaviour to men who work with teenagers, but it doesn't come naturally to them. A lot of men who work with teenagers want to show off, want to be seen, to teach and be visible. I show them how to just 'be', act as if they are at home, without showing off or drawing attention to themselves. This means the individuals come to them of their own volition, the teenagers come out of curiosity, learn by example, and learn by choice. That is one of the ways to teach teenagers, but there is so much more to say.

For now, let's contend ourselves with the statement, being an elder isn't simple, isn't commonplace, isn't taught in our society, but it is desperately needed. Let's go back to the Ugly Duckling, and see how he becomes an elder.

CHAPTER EIGHTEEN
THE LIMITERS OF OUR HORIZONS

The Story

Toward evening he came upon a poor little hut. It was so wretchedly crooked that it looked as if it couldn't make up its mind which way to fall and that was why it was still standing. The wind was blowing so hard that the poor little duckling had to sit down in order not to be blown away. Suddenly he noticed that the door was off its hinges, making a crack; and he squeezed himself through it and was inside.

An old woman lived in the hut with her cat and her hen. The cat was called Sonny and could both arch his back and purr. Oh yes, he could also make sparks if you rubbed his fur the wrong way. The hen had very short legs and that was why she was called Cluck Lowlegs. But she was good at laying eggs, and the old woman loved her as if she were her own child.

In the morning the hen and the cat discovered the duckling. The cat meowed and the hen clucked.

"What is going on?" asked the old woman, and looked around. She couldn't see very well, and when she found the duckling she thought it was a fat, full-grown duck. "What a fine catch!" she exclaimed, "Now we shall have duck eggs, unless it's a drake. We'll give it a try."

So the duckling was allowed to stay for three weeks on probation, but he laid no eggs. The cat was master of the house and the hen the mistress. They always referred to themselves as "we and the world," for they thought that they were half the world - and the better half at that. The duckling thought that he should be allowed to have a different opinion, but the hen did not agree.

"Can you lay eggs?" she demanded.

"No." answered the duckling.

"Then keep your mouth shut."

And the cat asked, "Can you arch your back? Can you purr? Can you make sparks?"

"No."

"Well, in that case, you have no right to have an opinion when sensible people are talking."

Interpretation of this part of the story

When I came to read the story as an allegory for a single parent boy, I started to feel this section was out of place. It didn't fit in my understanding of the passage from boy to man. Then I remembered the story is autobiographical. Hans Christian Andersen returned to school at the age of 17, suddenly, I understood. This is his return to school, the cat and hen are his teachers. The hen is a self-important teacher who has been given the chance to lord it over all her young wards. The hen teaches conformity, this is the simple way of getting through life, don't dream too much. I can just imagine the 17 year-old Andersen talking enthusiastically about his wish to become a writer and the teachers trying to put him in his place.

Resonance for us now

The hen and cat have been given a position of responsibility and they are convinced they know best, truly believing they are the better half of the world. They parody all the people who think they know how the world is run, and who scorn anyone who thinks differently. The hen lays eggs – that is her soul's purpose, she is happy and content doing it. She has found what she is good at. The cat arches his back, purrs and makes sparks, again these things make him happy and content. They are both correct in feeling these things are important, but they are both very wrong in believing that everyone should do the same. This is the damaging advice we have all received from friends and foes alike – *'it worked for me, so, it must work for you.'* Their lives are content and fulfilled, this surely must look very appealing to the Ugly Duckling, but he also knows he can not be part of this cosy picture, he is not like them. The more they try to make him become like them the more distressing it must be.

There is another factor at play here. The hen and cat live in abject poverty. They live in a wretched crooked hut. Despite this they are awfully pleased with themselves. There is a deal of self-delusion. Maybe they are so content and complacent because they don't want to be confronted with their own reality. They live in poverty, and despite it, they continue to believe they are fine. There is a feeling of staleness, sticking with what we've got, stagnation.   A lot of teachers feel this way.

Examples from near and far

When I left Art College in the early 1980's I said to my tutors and peers.
"I want a job which combines working in the community and creativity".
Many of them said to me-
'That's not possible, you can't do it, you'll never earn enough money, you need to sell work through Galleries and Museums.'

Their advice was well intentioned, they thought they were saving me from going down a blind alley. They had no experience of doing the work I wanted to do yet they gave their advice. I enjoyed working in the community and I enjoyed being creative. I knew it was possible, they didn't. It wasn't a blind alley, like many other people at the time, I took a risk, ignored their views, and it worked out fine. The combination of creativity and community work is now one of the quickest growing cultural industries in Britain. It is a multi-million pound employer of hundreds of artists, with tens of thousands of people participating each year. It is much more financially viable than selling work through galleries and museums. If I'd followed their advice I would have gone down a blind alley. Somehow the hen ended up in a blind alley, and is in denial about it. The only way to ignore this fact is to bluster and browbeat those she feels are inferior or not as good as herself.

How can we use this?
On a personal level

The hen and cat are also internal to the Ugly Duckling. All too often in our interpretations of myths and fairy tales, we tend to externalize the characters. The good is within us and the bad tends to be seen as outside us. However, as with all stories the messages are internal as well external. The Ugly Duckling believes he's ugly. He has more than likely also taken onboard more messages, we all do. It shows how the process is ongoing. I see this as the next stage of the internal messages, it is a sort of internal peer pressure – *'other people are like this, so I should do it too'*. It is a very tough message and a difficult one to counteract. You need to be strong to rise above such peer pressure. We are surrounded by these messages. These messages become part of us, we adopt and adapt. We need to question such internal and external messages.

If we are to become elders

A man found an eagle's egg and put it in a nest of a barnyard hen. The eagle hatched with the brood of chicks and grew up with them.

All his life the eagle did what the barnyard chicks did, thinking he was a barnyard chicken. He scratched the earth for worms and insects. He clucked and cackled. And he would thrash his wings and fly a few feet into the air.

Years passed and the eagle grew very old. One day he saw a magnificent bird above him in the cloudless sky. It glided in graceful majesty among the powerful wind currents, with scarcely a beat of its strong golden wings.

The old eagle looked up in awe. "Who's that?" he asked.

"That's the eagle, the king of the birds," said his neighbour. "He belongs to the sky. We belong to the earth – we're chickens." So the eagle lived and died a chicken, for that's what he thought he was. ★9

CHAPTER NINETEEN
IN THE FLOW

The Story

The duckling was sitting in the corner and was in a bad mood. Suddenly he recalled how lovely it could be outside in the fresh air when the sun shone; a great longing to be floating in the water came over the duckling, and he could not help talking about it.

"What is the matter with you?" asked the hen as soon as she had heard what he had to say. "You have nothing to do, that's why you get ideas like that. Lay eggs or purr, and such notions will disappear."

"You have no idea how delightful it is to float in the water, and to dive down to the bottom of a lake and get your head wet." said the duckling.

"Yes, that certainly does sound amusing," said the hen. "You must have gone mad. Ask the cat - he is the most intelligent being I know - ask him whether he likes to swim or dive down to the bottom of a lake. Don't take my word for anything … Ask the old woman, who is the cleverest person in the world; ask her whether she likes to float and to get her head all wet."

"You don't understand me!" wailed the duckling.

"And if I don't understand you, who will? I hope you don't think that you are wiser than the cat or the old woman - not to mention myself. Don't give yourself airs! Thank your Creator for all He has done for you. Aren't you sitting in a warm room among intelligent people whom you *could learn something from? While you, yourself, do nothing but say a lot of nonsense and aren't the least bit amusing! Believe me, that's the truth, and I am only telling it to you for your own good. That's how you recognize a true friend; it's someone who is willing to tell you the truth, no matter how unpleasant it is. Now get to work: lay some eggs, or learn to purr and arch your back."*

"I think I'll go out into the wide world," replied the duckling.

"Go right ahead!" said the hen.

Interpretation of this part of the story

This represents the fifth stage of his rites of passage, his connection to a purpose in life. He has spent time with other youngsters and they have failed to help him. He has now spent time with some older people and they too have failed to help him. But in this failure there is a success, he is able to become angry and re-connect with his joy, back to who he actually is.

For the first time in the whole story the Ugly Duckling is angry, in a bad mood. Thus far he has pretty much accepted everything life has thrown at him. However, something changes. He gets into a bit of a rage. This is a good thing, because it means he is defending himself against the onslaught of external and internal messages. Our society sees anger as damaging and dangerous, this doesn't have to be the case. Often a good burst of rage can clear the air, allows us to express our frustrations in a new, more concise manner, and actually move things forward.

Here we have a defining moment in the Ugly Ducklings life. It is such an important statement, and it is such a good guide to us all on how to be. By continually being confronted by the hen, and spending a long time trying to lay eggs (haven't we all been in those jobs!) he becomes angry, not compliant, not trying to please, and at that instant he remembers. He remembers the 'something', and connects with how lovely it was. *"How delightful it is to float in the water, and to dive down to the bottom of the lake and get your head wet."* He has remembered what makes him happy, he re-connects to his path. He remembers an activity giving him joy, something he wants to do with all his heart. Until this moment his life has been full of despair and misery. He has tried to conform, he has tried to fit in, he has even adopted the label Ugly Duckling, that's how far he has bent over. But, by connecting with something bringing him joy, he is reminded of who he is, not what his mother taught him.

> *When he puts his head in the water he isn't ugly, he isn't tough.*
> *He survives through love.*
> *He is in his rightful place.*
> *When he puts his head under water he doesn't have to be hard.*
> *He isn't just getting through life, he is actually living.*
> *He is in the flow of his life.*

Resonance for us now

The older chicken, as a teacher, tries to put the pupil in his place, using all the usual tricks of the trade. I know most teachers are desperately trying to cope with a tide of children needing specialist development and care. I know that the vast majority perform a brilliant job. To teach the next generation should be the most wonderfully creative job in the world, it should attract only the best and most imaginative people. We have arranged our society in such a way that the majority of our teachers are limiters – limiters of damage, limiters of imagination, limiters of our horizons.

How many times have we come across people who have said *"I am only telling it to you for your own good."* The teacher who thinks he knows best, the parent who is trying to suppress spontaneity, the work colleague who wants to remind you of the pecking order. All such advice is given with an agenda. Their advice, their guidance and 'wisdom' comes from their limited personal experience. They can see no further than their own world, their own existence, and can't relate to someone else's. They want to retain control, and not let anything change. When this approach hasn't been effective in restoring order the hen tries a different tack. You are amongst you elders and betters, you should be grateful for their indulgence. *"Don't give yourself airs"*. Your betters and elders don't want to get their heads wet, so why should you. It's a convincing argument for those of us who want to conform, who believe we are happy with the way things are. The Ugly Duckling is deeply unhappy about how things are, he is not afraid of change, he's in the middle of a rites of passage, so it doesn't work.

Finally, the lonely one is being offered friendship, probably for the first time in his life. *"That's how you recognize a true friend; it's someone who is willing to tell you the truth, no matter how unpleasant it is."* The offer of friendship is conditional, it is conditional on him laying eggs or arching his back, and he knows he'll never do that. Besides, he has had a brief glimpse of his soul's purpose, now he needs to pursue something. He knows what he is seeking, for the first time he feels a sense of purpose.

Going with the flow

Many millions of us are in the wrong job, in the wrong relationship, in the wrong country, whatever. We know this is true, but we kid ourselves everything is OK. We conform and attempt to earn a living whilst being unhappy, this leaves us always seeking something indefinable, we know something is missing. We ignore and suppress our anger, frustration and confusion. Then maybe someone says something in innocence, and we fly off the handle, react very strongly. These are important moments.

It is the moment in which the Ugly Duckling starts to take control of his life. Instead of allowing the hen to dictate to him how he should be, what he should do, he starts to think for himself. He remembers when he was happy, content, and able to do what he needed to do. He remembers when he was able to achieve a task with a minimum of effort.

*"You yourself are in an ecstatic state to such a point that you feel as though you almost don't exist. I've experienced this time and again. My hand seems devoid of myself, and I have nothing to do with what is happening. I just sit there watching in a state of awe and wonderment. And it just flows out of me."*10

When we feel like this we are at peace with the world, we can seemingly achieve very difficult tasks effortlessly. Many (hopefully all) of us have experienced being in the flow. It is described as performing at your peak and stretching beyond former limits. There are so many different ways of achieving this state - by playing music, doing athletics, yoga, doing arts or crafts, solving mathematical problems, whatever. It is a state of self-forgetfulness - the opposite of thoughtfulness. When we are unhappy and in the wrong job, we find it very difficult to feel this way. When we are content and happy with life we can be in the flow all day, if we are lucky enough. We can also experience micro-flows, small bursts of being in the right place every day- indeed we need to seek such experiences. When you are in the flow you can master your addictions, you can get above them. Many people say they suddenly realized hours have passed, and yet it seems like just a few minutes. These are all indications as to the location of your soul's purpose. The more times we experience them the closer we are getting to knowing who we are, and what we really should be doing.

If we don't follow our calling we will become stuck and unable really have a happy life, we become dependent on others to fulfill us.

*"Your vitality is your destiny; it defines you and allows you to be creative. It is your job to cooperate with it. If you don't do your part finding a place for all your strength and promise, it will transform. Instead of being receptive to the constant invitations to increase the life in you, you will start being submissive to other people. The object of your surrender will shift from life itself to a particular person or group of persons."*11

The Ugly Duckling leaves. He leaves on his terms. Instead of allowing fate to blow him from pillar to post, he has made a decision, he has willingly stepped into the wider world. In terms of his rites of passage he has declared how much he wants the experience, he is seeking his fate, not just passively accepting it. He is drawing the experience to him, and that is so important, he is taking responsibility for his life.

Examples from near and far

You're lazy and idle because you aren't working. This message is such a familiar one. It is a hopelessly inappropriate message, and we all seem very keen to give it to our teenagers. When we say these things they seem to make sense, but when we actually take time to think about their natural conclusion we see how perverse they are. Keep busy, work is good, it doesn't matter whether you like the work, or if you are any good at it, just be in a job. So many families I know are built in this way. Please consider this the next time you make a quick and simple judgment about a teenager who is stewing in his room, apparently not doing anything. Consider the possibly he hasn't got a clue about what he wants to do with his life, and he is so bereft of inspiration and creativity he is now unable to move. Your responsibility is not to nag him, not to push him into a meaningless and menial job that will have little or no value. Your responsibility is to inspire him, to be a positive role model for him, show him what it is to be inspired and creative.

Don't know how to do that? Don't worry you are not alone. Our present governments, those we have elected to make our decisions for us, are desperate to get everyone into a job. They are fixated on this aim, because once you are there, they can ignore you. If everyone is in a job, regardless of how menial, how depressing it is, then our governments are happy, and we should be. I don't think so! We have all bought into this concept. I constantly come up against this in my work. I'm supposed to be supporting people back into work, and with the majority of them they have little or no education, few qualifications, often minimal literacy or reading ability. However, some of them earn many hundreds of pounds each week through drugs and other illegal activities. I, and many others, suggest they would be 'better off' stacking shelves in a supermarket for £50 per week. Their reaction is correct, roughly translated, *'you must be joking!'* Where is the adrenaline rush stacking shelves? Where is the thrill being told what to do by other people? Why should we have to go to work really early in the morning? How proud can you feel in such a job? I'm not saying everyone should be involved in illegal activities. What I do know is we have to compete with the adrenaline rush, and the only way to compete is to work with the entrepreneurial spirit, try to divert it into community benefit projects. That is a tough job.

How can we use this?
On a personal level
Remember, just because someone is a teacher it doesn't mean they know the truth about you. Try to extrapolate some of the external messages those teachers might have given you during your school years, you may well have internalized them. Re-examine them.

You can't draw
You're no good at sports
Don't bother with him, he's stupid
They are not true!

Maybe, because a teacher told you something, you have made a bad career choice. When I say teacher, I mean not just those in our schools, but those older people we have met or allowed to influence us, who should have know better!

I can accept we need to do the wrong jobs in order to know what is the right one. It is good to experience diversity in life. I certainly had enough jobs I didn't enjoy, but I also didn't stay in them for a long time. There are millions of us in the wrong job, and too many of us are kidding ourselves that we are OK. Often we knew in the first few minutes it was wrong, but years later we are still hanging in there - because we need the money, because we are too old to change, because our family need us to stay there, whatever. There are a million and one reasons, and all of them are wrong, and we know it. It is a true privilege to be born as a human being, we are remarkable, unique individuals who are capable of so much. It is never too late to connect to who you should be. Indeed it is your duty as a human being to find what you are good at, and try to earn a living through it. Otherwise you end up being old, embittered, full of regrets, what-if's.

If we are to become elders

The hen believes she is an elder, but her inflexibility shows her immaturity. She believes she has made the right choice and she has stuck at that choice for a very long time. Maybe when she first made the choice it was correct, and maybe she was actually a good teacher then. However, it was a long, long time ago. As we grow older, we change- our needs and abilities change too. I'm not saying they have to, but they may well do. She has remained in the same place for too long. We shouldn't end up having to justify ourselves in our abject poverty as she does.

So, an elder doesn't ever think he's got it sussed. When you find your niche, enjoy it, but don't think you now needn't do any more learning or training, because that really makes you ugly!

CHAPTER TWENTY
VISION QUEST

The Story

And the duckling left. He found a lake where he could float in the water and dive to the bottom. There were other ducks, but they ignored him because he was so ugly.

Interpretation of this part of the story

This represents the sixth stage of his rite. He is again striking out on his own, but this time with an intent, with purpose, this is a vision quest. The Ugly Duckling strikes out under his own steam, he makes a decision to ignore the messages of his mother, his siblings, his teachers, to see what he is capable of achieving by himself. For me he is now in his thirties, he is able to make more mature decisions and capable of deciding his own fate. He is moving towards becoming a self-made man. We have a lot of self-made men around, and we'll discuss how effective they are later. For now, he finds a lake and claims it as his own. He indulges his soul's purpose, he puts his head under water. He has created a space for himself, and here he will enter the next stage of initiation, he will undertake a vision quest. He doesn't do it consciously, but he is drawn to it by his decision to ignore the others. He is starting to reject the messages he has been given, and he is seeking to find whom he really is. He is on his own, he is completely alone, and he will feel very lonely. This can be very depressing, but it is also necessary. Here he will become self-reliant.

Resonance for us now

Paradoxically, by being alone the boy can return to his community, knowing why he needs to be with others, and knowing the gifts he can share. In all indigenous rites of passage for boys, there is a period during which the initiate is on his own. He shares his experience on his return with the elders who help him to interpret it, support him, and they bless and honour him for his work. This must be done. It confirms who he is. The wider community recognizes and honours him for who he is, and there is a dependency implicit in this. A man can only become a man when he is recognized as such by elders and the community.

This relates to the concept of self-made men. At present we have built a myth in our culture about the importance of being a self-made man. It links directly back to the mothers' initial message *"he can look after himself."* Men believe they are alone in the world. They are suffering from their parental betrayal, which drives them into ascent. In this ascent they create huge businesses and corporations, this represents their drive, their loneliness, their anger.

I set up a company in 1981, which started as a small group of friends bringing art to deprived communities. Working from our hearts. As the years went by, we grew, we became famous, we expanded. In 1993 we were employing ten people full time, we worked all over Europe, we were a success. At that time the Arts Council of Wales asked to appraise our work. They conceded they didn't have the expertise to do so, but could I suggest someone? I was furious–
'There isn't anyone who can do that, no one has achieved what we have achieved, so how can anyone judge us.'
I was serious, I believed I was a self-made man, and my business was unique. They persisted, and I agreed on one man, Chris Elphick, who was ten years older than I,

and whom I respected. The terrified Arts Council officers ushered him into my presence and waited to see what happened. Chris calmly took all my rage, my indignation, and listened. He agreed, I was right. Then as I talked he identified little things, certain traits, which I was unaware of. I listened to him and learnt. He honoured me, he listened to me and praised me. I realized I wasn't a self-made man, I was reliant on a huge network of people to support and sustain me. I realized I didn't have to prove anything anymore. Within two years the business was much reduced, was again working from the heart, remembering why we set up in the first place. All those men who don't find their mentors, who don't connect to elders with wisdom, continue to feed the ravenous appetites of their corporations, and they loose connection with their indigenous natures. They are not captains of finance, they are shallow, immature children, unable to rest and take time out to reflect on what is important, what really is of value. Sir Isaac Newton is quoted as saying his outstanding contributions to science were made whilst *"standing on the shoulders of giants"*. Whether this was an ironic statement or not, is unimportant. It is a principle we all need to acknowledge, we need the support of others, nothing we create or achieve is in a vacuum, no one is entirely alone and without support. If only the Ugly Duckling knew this!

Examples from near and far

The vision quest is another complex device our ancestors comprehended, they were able to use it as and when needed. At moments of crisis, when a particular problem seemed impenetrable, when all else has failed. It is not something for the faint hearted, or the undecided, it should be undertaken by the committed. In Chapter Two we discussed the importance of being a 'knower of nature', and the vision quest is the culmination of this. The Ugly Duckling has been in nature for some time, and he is starting to master it. He has sought a deepening of himself, and this is reflected in his relationship to nature. Vision quest is magical, there is no other word to describe it. However much you may think you know, when you undertake this properly you will experience something beyond your comprehension. As a master of the physical world the Ugly Duckling is about to experience the metaphysical. The principle here is to focus the individual on who he is, and what he is about. By focusing and developing himself, he reaches a concentrated place, able to endure loneliness.

This process enables the individual to be alone in nature. He has to feel at one with nature, and by doing so, he will come across a sign, an indication. If he is astute enough, he will see it and be able to work with it. I don't feel there is the time or space to discuss the exact details of vision quest here, but, for those who are unaware, here are some bare bones.

"Most vision quests last for up to three or four days and nights.
During the time the initiate is alone, and fasting, he is allowed water and a few survival items.
He is equipped with ceremonial tools and symbolic items of importance to him.

He is at risk....because he knows this he tends to act conservatively, mindful of the sanctity of life in his body as he outwardly enacts the personal terms of his quest.

He will create a 'power place' and he will hold a wakeful vigil at various times, including the last night of his threshold ordeal.

When three or four days and nights are over, he will return to the secular world of the base camp, where the midwife waits for him.

He will have a story to tell.

*It is up to the midwife to hear this story clearly and to point out its salient points to him."*12*

Taken from The Roaring of the Sacred River by Steven Foster and Meredith Little.

For me, our young people are doing this work, they are stepping out into the wilderness, but they lack support. Like the Ugly Duckling they lack the last vital sentence *"It is up to the midwife to hear this story clearly and to point out its salient points to him."* The job the elders do when the young person returns from his quest. They listen and interpret his story with the benefit of their accumulated knowledge. Not judgmentally, not condescendingly, but in a way which honours and respects what has happened.

How can we use this?

We can only be self reliant, if we know who we are, what our soul's purpose is- we need to have been to the darkest and most fearful places in our soul to find it. We need to ask a question, create a space in nature, make it our own, be alone, be with ourselves, and then see what happens. Not try to work it out in the mind. Listen to nature, watch nature, and then something will happen.

This is a spiritual experience - it is not religious. Throughout time immemorial such work has been supervised and managed by the elders for the initiates. This has nothing to do with a particular religion or spiritual path, all religions and paths lead to this place.

"And it came to pass in those days, that Jesus
came from Nazareth of Galilee,
and was baptized of John in Jordan...
And immediately the Spirit driveth him into the wilderness.
And he was there in the wilderness forty days, tempted of Satan:
And was with the wild beasts; and the angels ministered unto him."
-The Gospel of Mark

"Now scorched, now froze, in forest dread, alone,
naked and fireless, set upon his quest,
the hermit battles, purity to win."
-The Buddha, Majjhima-nikava, XII

"Then he came to love solitude, so he used to go off to a cave in Hira where he would practice prayers (tahannuth) certain nights before returning to his family. Then he would come back to his family and take provisions for the like number of nights until unexpectedly the truth came to him."
– Islam, Muhammad and His Religion

We all need to do this work, without confronting ourselves we will remain childish and immature. There is no short cut, this has to be done. When we undertake a vision quest we are admitting that we have a problem, we are desperately seeking help, things have definitely come to a head. Many people do this by going to a therapist. In the therapy sessions they are able to talk about their past, their relationships, and during this period of 'confession', they are able to come to a clearer understanding of their underlying patterns of behaviour. By confessing and having this mirrored they are able to maybe see how they have abused themselves, how they absorbed false images and labels throughout their lives. This can lead to a better understanding and more compassionate view of the self. A vision quest does the same. Many see seeking help from a therapist as an admission of failure, as somehow being a retrospective step. It is not, therapy, vision quests, similar experiences are just opportunities to break through not break down. By seeking the help of a therapist or a vision quest we are admitting the things we have put off can no longer be put off.

*"I had finally reached the place of despair I had avoided feeling my entire life. It was as if all my relationships had been drawing me closer to experiencing that darkest of inner places. I knew it was time for me to learn to love and care for that wounded child within me."*13

Men need to listen to this message
As men, we need to remember we are not alone
We need to see how our parents or carers provided a basis for us
How that basis may have been in abuse and adversity, it is still the basis from which we have created our life
We all need to be thankful for our origins however humble or sorrowful they may have been
As men, we need to see how many other people love and support us, despite the fact that we didn't ask them to!
Bless them and thank them for their support
Don't turn down sincere offers of help, learn to receive as well as give
As men, we need to stop trying to prove something
Take our time, reflect and be honest
Ask for help, be collaborative, share our knowledge and wealth
As men, we need to cry and grieve

CHAPTER TWENTY-ONE
THE DISTANT SWANS

The Story

Autumn came and the leaves turned yellow and brown, then they fell from the trees. The wind caught them and made them dance. The clouds were heavy with hail and snow. A raven sat on a fence and screeched, "Ach! Ach!" because it was so cold.

When just thinking of how cold it was is enough to make one shiver, what a terrible time the duckling must have had.

One evening just as the sun was setting gloriously, a flock of beautiful birds came out from among the rushes. Their feathers were so white that they glistened; and they had long, graceful necks. They were swans. They made a very loud cry, then they spread their powerful wings. They were flying south to a warmer climate, where the lakes were not frozen in the winter. Higher and higher they circled. The ugly duckling turned round and round in the water like a wheel and stretched his neck up toward the sky; he felt a strange longing. He screeched so piercingly that he frightened himself.

Oh, he would never forget those beautiful birds, those happy birds. When they were out of sight the duckling dived down under the water to the bottom of the lake; and when he came up again he was beside himself. He did not know the name of those birds or where they were going, and yet he felt that he loved them as he had never loved any other creatures. He did not envy them. It did not even occur to him to wish that he were so handsome himself. He would have been happy if the other ducks had let him stay in the henyard: that poor, ugly bird!

Interpretation of this part of the story

Despite leaving the farmyard, he has always been with other birds until this recent time. On his own, he is seeking contemplation, reflection, and then absorption of the mirrored images from nature. He is asking the question *"Who am I......Am I an Ugly Duckling?"* And into the silence following the asking of that question, comes the response.

The raven

The raven is a very remarkable bird, why does he mention it? Hans Christian Andersen would have known about the druidic and symbolic significance of the raven. He is linked to Bran the Blessed whose head is buried under the Tower of London. All those storytellers knew of the special qualities of the raven, and how to be around it.

"One day a man passing through a wood heard a raven calling. When he was near enough, the raven said
'I am a princess by birth, and I am bewitched, but you can deliver me from the spell.'
'What must I do?' Asked the man
'Go farther into the woods.' Said she."
The Brothers Grimm, "The Raven"

The raven offers initiation, protection and the gift of prophecy, all of which the Ugly Duckling needs, and is seeking right now. The raven travels from one world to the other, his appearance marks the death of one thing and the birth of another. He is able to

128

pass into the next world, drawing up the darkness and the potentially destructive aspects of the psyche.

"The raven's association with death becomes an association with depth and thus with deep psychology and the transformative powers of initiation - for such a moment marks to a greater or lesser extent the death of the old self, and the rebirth of a new self."★14

Resonance for us now

He sees swans flying in the distance. What an experience for the Ugly Duckling. He has made a decision to be on his own, he has self-determined for the first time in his life. Having created the space, something magical happens. There for the first time in his life he sees a swan. He is inspired, in awe, and he doesn't know why. He screams loudly in response to their calls, he doesn't understand how he can do that. *"He loved them as he had never loved any other creatures."* This is what often happens on a vision quest, you experience unexpected things, things don't make sense, but resonate deep in your body. You are confronted by aspects of yourself you haven't experienced before. You are able to do this, because you are not surrounded by other people. It may not make immediate sense, but the experience needs to be worked with, absorbed, reflected upon and developed. Then at some point it will make sense.

He sees the swans flying above him, in the distance, he seems them briefly, for a moment, and yet that moment will remain with him throughout his life. For me the swans represent older men, the elders. He is only able to catch a brief glimpse of them, they represent an idealized version of the truth. When we see things in the distance we can often believe them to be better than they really are.

This is a problem in men's work at present, the elders of whom, I, and many others, speak are mythological, and the reality can be a let down. Young men are seeking wisdom keepers and in the search they create idealized versions of what they want. The concept of an elder is not being fulfilled in reality. Unfortunately, most of the older men I know are still immature- they lack wisdom and humility. This is a familiar tale for many men. The role models on offer can be grouchy moaners who have a very sour point of view. As a conscquence many younger men don't want to become old, especially if this is all there is on offer. It isn't, and it doesn't have to be like that. So long as we realize what is happening here, we can deal with it. The swans represent his ideals about elders. They are absolutely perfect, by seeing them, by becoming conscious of their existence, even if it maybe imagined, the Ugly Duckling has manifested something he can strive towards.

Examples from near and far

My own experience of this has been to meet many highly acclaimed spiritual leaders, to befriend them, to have close and intimate contact with them. By becoming close I have been able to observe their very humanness, their weaknesses, and their failings. That was initially a disappointment, I felt let down, but then I realized my initial expectation was for them to have transcended normality, they hadn't. Instead of this realization being a disappointment it has become an encouragement. I now know that I too can strive towards the impossible goal of transcending my anger, jealousy, petty mindedness, just like everyone else on the planet. As young men we all need to set ourselves standards and targets and try to attain them, but very rarely will we achieve them. The Ugly Duckling has seen an ideal, he has created a belief system, he has created something to believe in. This is a vital step towards his survival of the winter. When we step into despair, when we reach the very lowest ebb, we need to have distant dimly remembered dream to cling to.

How can we use this?
On a personal level
Spend time in nature
Don't just go for a walk, find a place in nature in which you are unobserved and feel at home
Stay there
Stay there longer than you intended
See what happens

Try to work on problems in the abstract, not literally. Take an issue out into the woods and leave it there symbolically. See what the answer is, it may be in the wind, in the sunshine, the actions of a bird, try not to judge.

If you really want to do a vision quest and feel committed enough to see it through then you will need to search for instructors and courses. I undertook one on Dartmoor, it transformed my life, and I bless and thank everyone who held and nurtured me through the process. It was a very wonderful combination of freedom to express myself, to explore who I am, whilst being held, knowing I was safe amongst people who knew what they were doing. It was also incredibly difficult, scary and made me very ill - not easy, nor simple. The vision quest I undertook was at a pivotal moment in my life, it came at a time when I was uncertain about everything in my life, particularly my long-term relationship. By undertaking the vision quest, and fully throwing myself into it, I was able to come up with a clear and undeniable truth about myself. I didn't want to be in the relationship any more. In that sense this conclusion represented the flight of swans for me. They brought about huge and destructive changes in mine and my families' lives, the consequences of which I am still dealing with. But, I know it was the truth, I have an unshakable faith and belief in that decision because of how I came to it.

If we are to become elders
We need to recognize the importance of this kind of life transforming experience, and to seek it out. Not to just remain in our comfort zone, but to reach outwards and be held in the endeavour. Not to seek it as a thrill or an adventure to tick off a list, but to use it to deepen our understanding of our own soul.

I know such experiences can transform lives, so please do this work with respect and understand such things need to be fully participated in and only undertaken when absolutely necessary.

CHAPTER TWENTY-TWO
DARK NIGHTS OF THE SOUL

The Story

The weather grew colder and colder. The duckling had to swim round and round in the water, to keep just a little space for himself that wasn't frozen. Each night his hole became smaller and smaller. On all sides of him the ice creaked and groaned. The little duckling had to keep his feet constantly in motion so that the last bit of open water wouldn't become ice.

Interpretation of this part of the story

He has sought help, he has spent time with his peers, he has spent time with elders, and now in his solitude, he comes to some kind of solace and contentment. This represents the seventh stage of his rite of passage. It is the descent after the initial ascent. The Ugly Duckling is now maybe in his 40's. We are in the deepest winter, there is very little sunshine, very little warmth, the world has turned dark. In these times we become retrospective, introverted, we look into ourselves, and confront our depths. We are not full of sunshine and lightness, we are in the dark, and there is a grim finality to this stage. The Ugly Duckling is now close to the end. The end of everything - he is coming to the end of his rites of passage, and he is increasingly close to death. He is aware of this looming darkness, he chooses to turn towards it, not reject it. There is surrender implicit in this passage. He is keeping himself busy, he is keeping his feet in motion. As described before, these are our furious attempts to keep occupied, to stay in work, to be seen to be of use.

Resonance for us now

This is the descent inevitably following the ascent, this is winter inevitably following summer. When we align our bodies and souls with our land, and the seasons, we are deeply connected. So, as the winter comes on we prepare ourselves for death, for the inevitable death, which we know will lead to re-birth. When we are in tune with the seasons we know there will be a Spring following on from Winter. The Ugly Duckling knows this and so he faces the oncoming darkness with humble elegance. He is not resigned to his fate, he is drawing it to him. He has faith in himself, in the world and in the bigger picture, he acknowledges the possibility of death.

"Death is an appropriate image. And that is exactly what it is, an image. It doesn't mean you are going to die, although you may feel the sadness of ending in the midst of your dark night. It means that life wants to go on differently. Real, vital life doesn't repeat itself." ★15

When we live at the pace we live we forget this. We become fearful about death, winter, darkness, because we live too fast. We've forgotten that life leads to death. We keep busy, we paddle our pools furiously, pretending such things are important. As we do this we ignore the changing seasons and the lessons they bring. We are trying to stay in the summer sunshine all the time- this isn't useful.

An essential element of winter is the cold. When the land freezes the cold kills the accumulated organisms and bacteria of the summer. The frost regenerates the land. The cold of winter is a healing force for change. Yet, as a culture we have rejected the

134

cold, we have forced it out of our lives. A woman friend told how she wanted to buy a thick wooly jumper during the winter, and went in pursuit of such in the shops of the city. There were none. We live in centrally heated houses, we travel to work in heated cars, and we work in heated offices. We no longer have any need to wrap up warm against the cold.

The majority of the densely populated countries of the world are remarkably blessed with very clearly defined seasons. Our attempts to avoid this truth by heating our houses, by surrounding ourselves with the orange glow of our cities, deny us our heritage. Our heritage is to be aligned with the seasons, to love their different moods and feelings. The Spring is about new growth, nurturing fresh shoots; the Summer is about growth, expansion, fullness; the Autumn is about abundance, about harvest; and the Winter is about introversion, about restoration, about composting. We are remarkably lucky to have such a diversity of seasons, and we need to appreciate what a privilege it is to live here. When we are in tune, we can accept the winter, accept the darkness and cold.

The Ugly Duckling is outside our comfortable houses, he is in the marshlands beyond our boundaries, and the rules which apply there are different. They are fierce, frightening, and awesome. They are also full of love and compassion. One of the rules there is you must have faith. Faith in yourself, in the bigger picture, faith in fate, faith in the unknowable. We are part of nature, and we have lost our faith in nature. We have disconnected with the interconnect-ness of everything. By not knowing whom we are, and what role we have in life, we have lost contact and therefore we are seeking to regain control. In our present state we are desperately seeking to be in charge, to know what is going on. We overheat our lives, we spend all our time attempting to pre-empt fate, seeking mastery of it all. Science tries to explain it all, it can't. You are never in total control, so let go. There is a plan, but when you try to know the plan, it disappears. The plan is that the seasons come and go whether you are around or not, they did this before you were born, and they will continue for millions of years after you have died.

Examples from near and far

This simple understanding is expressed in so many different ways by indigenous people:-

*   *in their honouring of the spirits*
*   *in their connection to the unknown, unseen, worlds*
*   *in the belief of our connection to everything*
*   *in their acceptance of life, death and illness*

They know about these things and they create rituals to make sure they remember them. Ritual and ceremony reminds us of who we are and at what stage the year is, such a vital function. There have been such markers for thousands of years, and they are connected to nature, to the unseen. We have to have faith in the invisible, in the world beyond ours, the one we have spent the last two hundred years trying to ignore and mitigate against. We can't mitigate against nature, we are part of it. When we accept this, we become part of a bigger, more generous world, one which can scare us, but will also look after us.

"And those who love their Mother, she never deserts them. As the hen protects her chickens, as the lioness her cubs, as the mother her newborn babe, so does the Earthly Mother protect the Son of Man from all danger and evils."★16

This is the true nature of being a human being. We are just a small part of an overall web, we are inter-dependent on the micro and macro aspects of the world, with everything which surrounds us. We are not alone, we never have been, we never will be. If we believe in this, then wonderful things will happen. We will be held by nature in a way scientists will never be able to measure. If we don't allow this into our lives, we create an empty and vacuous life - led cynically and desperately in our centrally heated, insulated environments - without hope, without faith, without imagination.

How can we use this?

★   *Encourage people to risk feeling down, depressed and ill, and actually take the time to recover properly.*

★   *The television is full of adverts for painkillers, suppressants which allow us to continue to be 'normal'. Encourage people not to take them. Avoid taking pills which say 'fast relief'.*

★   *Spend time in nature during the winter, not just the summer. Notice how beautiful it is.*

.

We need to acknowledge Winter. We tend to complain about it when the weather turns cold and snowy, it is also incredibly beautiful and magical. The inner child in each of us longs for a good deep snow each year, please don't forget how wonderful snow can be.

Stop trying to insulate our lives, stop turning up the thermometer on the heating, it will be good for the planet as well. Go out into the cold and appreciate it, I lived in a barn with just a wood burning stove in West Wales for two years, I know how delightful it can be! Being heated by wood fires is one of the most beautiful experiences which all human beings enjoy.

Slow down in winter, there is not such a need to rush around and be busy. It is dark a lot longer each day, so sleep longer. Sleeping longer, hibernating is natural, not lazy.

Take time to reflect and absorb the lessons of the previous year, winter is a time to think, reflect and learn from the previous months, time to take stock.

Mark and celebrate the winter solstice – the true birth of the New Year
We need to seek ways of accepting death. Stop ignoring it, we are surrounded
all the time.

See the positive in the negative. See the lessons in compost.

CHAPTER TWENTY-THREE
OUR DEEPEST FEARS

The Story

At last he was too tired to swim any more. He sat still. The ice closed in around him and he was frozen fast.

Early the next morning a farmer saw him and with his clogs broke the ice to free the duckling. The man put the bird under his arm and took it home to his wife, who brought the duckling back to life.

The children wanted to play with him. But the duckling was afraid that they were going to hurt him, so he flapped his wings and flew right into the milk pail. From there he flew into a big bowl of butter and then into a barrel of flour. What a sight he was!

The farmer's wife yelled and chased him with a poker. The children laughed and almost fell on top of each other, trying to catch him; and how they screamed! Luckily for the duckling, the door was open. He got out of the house and found a hiding place beneath some bushes, in the newly fallen snow; and there he lay so still, as though there were hardly any life left in him.

It would be too horrible to tell of all the hardship and suffering the duckling experienced that long winter. It is enough to know that he did survive.

Interpretation of this part of the story

The Ugly Duckling stops pretending, his feet stop paddling. At that moment, he is very close to death. He is in crisis both internally and externally. For me, in today's society, a great many men are in this place. These are fourty year old men who are confused about what they are doing with their lives. Maybe they are successful providers, but they are aware something is missing in their lives. They have been able to keep busy and avoid confronting this crisis, but at some point they have to crash and stop. For the Ugly Duckling the moment has arrived. Maybe he has faith in a God, maybe he doesn't, that isn't important – he just accepts his fate, he stops trying to be in control.

He is now in the eighth part of his rite of passage, he has to ask for help, and he asks for help from his elders. He is rescued by a man, by an older man. In a rite of passage, he is the elder who has been guiding the initiate invisibly throughout, and can see he now needs help. An elder is unobtrusive, doesn't lead with ego, leaves you to it, but also he tries to prevent you from dying. He helps just enough to get you through to the next stage without you being too obliged to him. Yet there is another stage to be endured, and this is one of the darkest and most difficult, the breaking of the ego.

Resonance for us now

"It is the pulling apart of meaning so that mystery can be revealed. It is the disappearance of an ego so that life can eventually move in its own time and its own way." ★17

The Ugly Duckling is saved, despite himself. He wasn't capable of living through the Winter, he needed someone to rescue him. He probably thought he would be able to survive the Winter on his own, but he wasn't. This is the breaking down of the ego. The ego in young boys is very strong- it is fed and fuelled by the disappointment of parental betrayal, and the ascent into the wilderness. We return to the self-made man, such a man has a large ego. Whilst he is in ascent he believes he is on his own. So many of the young men I work with feel isolated, bitter, alone and desperate. They have in a sense isolated themselves, but they have also never been shown how to live differently. Our teenagers don't know each generation does the same things, and has done the same thing for thousands of years. Our teenagers believe they are their own, deluded by their isolation, they enlarge their egos. They feed their egos by creating corporations, by being entrepreneurs, by being criminals, by exploring the very edges of the world as we know it.

> They are seeking boundaries, they don't find any:
> *Because we have abandoned them*
> *Because we don't have elders who can reign them in*
> *Because we forgot how to do this work*

What happens to the Ugly Duckling at this point is he is rescued by the most unlikely part of nature, a man. Someone he never dreamed would be of use to him. As a wild beast he more than likely is very scared of men, and yet it is the thing he fears the most which saves him. In this irony lies a humiliation. He is rescued and then covered in milk and flour -*"what a sight he was"*. The deflation of the ego, the descent is complete.

Without the ego he probably would have died many times before, I'm not denying the importance of the ego, it is a driving and powerful force for change. Bless it. But it is associated with the uninitiated. When we seek to pass through a rite of passage we need to go in one end full of ego, full of self-importance, and to come out the other, full of compassion, understanding and humility, to become self-confident. *How can we learn this?* The ego must be broken down, it doesn't die, it can't, but it needs to see the bigger picture. The bigger picture here for the Ugly Duckling is he can't make it through the winter without help. He is not alone. He is not invincible. He is vulnerable and needs to ask for help. He can't do this work by himself. We all need to learn this, reciprocity in action. For him this lesson is reinforced by the fact he has to rely on the one thing he fears the most for this assistance.

What a lesson! It's the things we reject, it's the people we hate, who are the ones capable of helping us the most. In addition for the Ugly Duckling there is the added humiliation of being covered in flour and being laughed at by the children, being chased by the wife, can his ego take such a bashing? How many of our proud self-made men could stand such a lesson? If they did they would be so much nearer to becoming whole human beings.

"It is the mind, the Ego, far more than outer circumstances, that creates our suffering." *18

When we learn to let go of the ego we learn that everything is actually alright, in it's right place, and we stop trying to manipulate the world.

The Ugly Duckling was humiliated by others in the farmyard he survived this through his mothers' love. When he was betrayed by his mother, he was deeply wounded and hurt. This hurt has created his identity- he is the Ugly Duckling. He has set off on a journey to find his true self. He has maybe rejected the Ugly Duckling, but still hasn't found who he truly is. Before he can do this he needs to be humiliated again, just one more time. This is a tough journey, but as we said earlier, rites of passage are not the soft option. He needs to learn he has to ask for help, he has to be assisted and guided, he is not able to make it on his own. By embracing his biggest fear, he realizes he can't make it through the winter on his own, he needs help. How many of the boys I work with need that lesson.

Everyone who has been to a very dark place, out on a dark night of the soul, knows how this feels. It is a deeply unhappy and lonely place, full of doubt, anguish and pain. It is as dark and miserable as can be, you loose your self, your ego, you go wild, you fall without ending, life is unbearable. It is also a huge blessing.

Examples from near and far

During the act of circumcision for the Samburu there is a huge amount of humiliation. The boys spend months being encouraged to be brash and openly aggressive, they strut and preen. Then, at the moment of circumcision they are publicly humiliated. They are surrounded by a mass of people, literally hundreds, some of whom they know, others they don't. These are the spectators, these are the witnesses- they witness the circumcision. The boy is held, firmly gripped by his elders, they forcibly control him. As the circumcisor makes his way round the village some boys quake uncontrollably, some literally leave their bodies, whilst others stand impassively like cows blankly observing the mounting crescendo of chaos around them. The moment arrives. He is brusquely stripped naked, water and milk poured over his head, he jumps down onto a spread cow skin at the shock of cold fluids. His legs are spread wide, everyone crowds in and gawps. Fights break out as people vie for the best views, there is no privacy, this is a very public display. For a people who never see each other naked, this is their darkest fear, this is a very frightening place. There is no hiding, despite being in a huge crowd, they are absolutely alone. The boys are watched, minutely observed from every angle, the crowd looks for flinching, or any displays of discomfort. This will bring dishonour onto their families, and they will be banned from village life if they cry out or show discomfort. He is cut and bleeds openly, then he is wrapped in the cow skin and carried into his ceremonial bed, there he can moan and groan. The next day the boys are either in bed or walking gingerly around the village. Their faces have been transformed, they are no longer brash and cocky, they are humble, they are very quiet. They have been publicly exposed and cut down to size, their humiliation is complete. For them, they have submitted themselves to the laws of their people. They have sacrificed their dignity for the good of their ancestors and elders. They have publicly committed themselves to their traditions and culture. They have demonstrated an ultimate act of respect -incomprehensible and alien to our Western mindset.

How can we use this?
On a personal level

When I was in my 40's I was running a very successful community arts business, I was being paid a huge wage, traveling the world, working with very exciting people. I had built the business up from scratch and I took a huge amount of pride from it. However, something happened, something changed. I knew if I kept my head down and continued to work in the way we had developed for another twenty years I would be fine. Everyone around me thought that was the best thing to do. I didn't. I quit. I gave the business to my younger colleagues and walked away. Something was missing and I knew I had to go and find it. For me this is a classic example of the change between being a 'father' and becoming an 'elder' about which I have already spoken. There is a need to offload the accumulative way of being and to develop a more expansive and less cluttered way of life. I also had my father as role model. He had worked very hard all his life right into his late 60's, and then retired. At the point of retiring he came to realize his whole existence was defined by work, being a journalist, he became old news, no-one wanted to know. In his retirement he became bitter and ill. I didn't want to go that way, the problem is, *what is the alternative?* A leap of faith.

If we are to become elders

Men need to admit their frailties and concerns
We all need to see the bigger picture
Stop trying to master nature, recognize that we don't know everything
See the magical and mysterious in everything around us
We need to accept we can't do everything by ourselves
Stop feeling we are alone, see what lesson we can learn from those people we don't like, see there is a lesson in everything we do, however small or insignificant it may seem
Ask for help, stop pretending to be an expert

Jump, brother, jump

CHAPTER TWENTY-FOUR
BECOMING OUR TRUE SELVES

The Story

When again the sun shone warmly and the larks began to sing, the duckling was lying among the reeds in the swamp. Spring had come!

He spread out his wings to fly. How strong and powerful they were!

Before he knew it, he was far from the swamp and flying above a beautiful garden. The apple trees were blooming and the lilac bushes stretched their flower-covered branches over the water of a winding canal.

Everything was so beautiful: so fresh and green.

Interpretation of this part of the story

The Ugly Duckling has survived the Winter. He has been through a huge amount of transformative experiences. He has mastered a great deal, and also been hurt, badly shaken, near to death, he has been through a rites of passage. The depth and breath of experience will be very useful in later life. He has certainly lived a full and exciting life thus far, and this range of experience - the good and the bad - has enabled him to grow strong and powerful. We forget this. We have a saying *'every cloud has a silver lining'*, and yet we seek to avoid the clouds. You don't experience the silver linings without the clouds! You don't become strong and powerful without experiencing disappointment and loss. He is initiated. He didn't do this by design, but he has come to this place anyway. He is so strong he can fly great distances easily. Again he is in his flow, and now he is returned to the place he left. He is not the same Ugly Duckling who left in autumn - he has been transformed. Because of his personal transformation, everything around him seems new and fresh, it is, it's Spring, he is in tune.

Resonance for us now

In many ways the story works as a quick and simple tale of one year, and in do-ing so we forget about time and age. For me he is now a lot older than a teenager. In our extremely fast and rapid lives we expect to reach maturity a lot faster than we actually do. Obviously, some very remarkable people reach this stage of life in their 20's, but they are very few and far between. I would say he is now in his late 40's or early 50's. Most men come to this place quite late in life compared to women. He is a much humbler man, he has learnt some very important lessons. Not only has he been through these experiences there is also a complicit acknowledgement here of his 'coming to terms' with events and himself. He has reached closure.

Examples from near and far

"Your pain is the breaking of the shell that encloses your understanding.

Even as the stone of the fruit must break, that its heart may stand in the sun, so must you know pain.

And could you keep your heart in wonder at the daily miracles of your life, your pain would not seem less wonderous than your joy;

And you would accept the seasons of your heart, even as you have accepted the seasons that pass over your fields.

And you would watch with serenity through the winters of your grief.
*Much of your pain is self-chosen."*19*

When we are through our rites of passage we know who are, we accept our lot, we can transcend the pain without blaming and anger, we just grieve it. We do this because we have been alone, alone in the wilderness. Then our thoughts turn back to the community we left, and how we can now integrate the lessons we have learnt. The Ugly Duckling has been initiated into manhood out in the flatlands, it is time to come home, to come back into his community.

How can we use this?
How do we reach closure?

Now there's a question. There are a multiplicity of answers. All I know is to have made mistakes, to admit to them, and to learn from them, which enables us to move on. For me a great many men are not admitting their mistakes, are not suffering humiliation, and are therefore still in ascent. Our culture looks to youth for its inspiration, this is wholly wrong. A mature and complete culture will always look to its elders for guidance. As individuals and as a society as a whole we need to now start to seek out our elders and ask them for help. This is an internal and external process, we need to seek our internal elder guidance as well.

Throughout the book I have given examples of rites of passage and rituals from other lands and peoples, please don't believe that I am therefore saying they are somehow 'better' than us. I use these examples because they remind us of something we forgot a while ago. Once we remember about this way of being, the solutions to our problems present themselves. I use them as examples of the way things could be in the future, not to romanticize our past. If the messages in this book have resonated within you then I know you are well on the way to creating the rituals and rites of passage which will be needed in the future.

Be the revolution that makes the revolution possible!

CHAPTER TWENTY-FIVE
WORTHY

The Story

Out of a forest of rushes came three swans. They ruffled their feathers and floated so lightly on the water. The ugly duckling recognized the birds and felt again that strange sadness come over him.

"I shall fly over to them, those royal birds! And they can hack me to death because I, who am so ugly, dare to approach them! What difference does it make? It is better to be killed by them than to be bitten by the other ducks, and pecked by the hens, and kicked by the girl who tends the henyard; or to suffer through the winter."

And he lighted on the water and swam toward the magnificent swans. When they saw him they ruffled their feathers and started to swim in his direction. They were coming to meet him.

"Kill me," whispered the poor creature, and bent his head humbly while he waited for death. But what was that he saw in the water? It was his own reflection; and he was no longer an awkward, clumsy, grey bird, so ungainly and so ugly. He was a swan!

It does not matter that one has been born in the henyard as long as one has lain in a swan's egg.

He was thankful that he had known so much want, and gone through so much suffering, for it made him appreciate his present happiness and the loveliness of everything about him all the more. The swans made a circle around him and caressed him with their beaks.

Interpretation of this part of the story

The Ugly Duckling is now in the ninth stage of his rite. He has accepted everything, he has come to terms with life. He has reached closure. He is now, for me, about 56 years old, he has been through a huge amount and his actions are those of an elder. He has achieved this despite his lack of male role models, which some would say mitigates against their necessity. I would just say he may well have reached this stage a lot earlier if he'd had elders around him, who knows.

I cried for a long time when I first read this passage, every time I read it, it stirs me, with its' awesome power and strength of feeling. The point at which he wants to kill himself, the act of bending down to accept death, is the point at which he sees his own beauty. He sees himself as a swan for the first time in the moment of resignation to his fate.

The Ugly Duckling bows his head. Bowing the head is a sign of respect, it is done to your elders and betters, he is honouring his ancestors, acknowledging their wisdom and beauty. In that moment there is no ego, he has recognized he needs help, he has recognized he doesn't know it all. He bends his head, and when we bend our head, we descend into grief. Grief comes after the humiliation. Grief accompanies humility and respect. Grief is a crucial and vital part of growing up for a human being. In Robert Bly's terms it is association with the accumulation of ashes.

"Ashes present a great diminishment away from the living tree with its huge crown and its abundant shade. The recognition of this diminishment is a proper experience for men who are

150

over thirty. If the man doesn't experience that diminishment sharply, he will retain his inflation, and continue to identify himself with all in him that can fly: his sexual drive, his mind, his refusal to commit himself, his addiction, his transcendence, his coolness. The coolness of some American men means that they have skipped ashes."★20

Resonance for us now

Young men are born with ovens in their bellies. They fuel these ovens with experience, ego, love and fear, everything is poured directly onto the flames. When we are young the fire burns with such intensity - everything is consumed, nothing remains. We burn brightly when we are in ascent. However, in descent, we slow down, we are remorseful, we are humiliated, we find humility. The fuel now turns to ashes. We accumulate ashes in our ovens- the burnt and absorbed transformative matter of our experience - in other words - wisdom. The ashes are also our ability to grieve. Grieving the transformation of the experience, grieving the passing of our youth, grieving the changes we cannot alter. Grieving not only our own lives, but for those of our ancestors, our families, our friends, our fellow travelers in the world. Oh, how we all need to grieve!

"People who do not know how to weep together are people who cannot laugh together. People who know not the power of shedding their tears together are like a time bomb, dangerous to themselves and to the world around them." ★21

If we don't learn how to grieve we will forever be young, forever be seeking something we don't know how to describe. When we don't grieve we absorb it into our bodies, the urge to grieve is so strong it has to go somewhere. It accumulates in our bodies, and eventually becomes illness, cancer, sickness, arthritis, so many diseases. The self-made man needs to grieve, if he doesn't he'll surely become ill and decrepit in later years. The Ugly Duckling is also learning he needs to grieve communally, amongst others. He is opening up with others, not on his own any more. He is starting the process of becoming an elder, and the only way to become an elder is to grieve the fact you are no longer young. He is becoming a role model, he is openly acting out grief, and he is now a strong and beautiful example to us all.

Examples from near and far

Hans Christian Andersen knew a lot about nature, so his choice of bird is careful. Swans remain as faithful couples throughout their lives, the males take a big part in the upbringing of the cygnets, much more than most other birds.

★   *They are tall and elegant, probably how he wished to see himself.*
★   *The swan amongst ducklings is a tall gangling stranger, just as he must have been when he went back to school. The swan represents his other-ness, his peculiarity, his ungainly-ness.*
★   *It also represents his sexuality, a dangerous peculiarity in those days, which was a liability. Yet, he persists in his other-ness and in the end it becomes his strength, from his strangeness comes the rich flow of stories by which he makes his way.*

151

He was born to be a writer and I am sure many people tried to put him off. He was always convinced he could become a writer, and had to overcome many obstacles to achieve his goal. He knew he was a writer, it was his souls' purpose. He is seeking positive male role models, and these are older men. One day he sees them off in the distance, flying, and this is just a brief view. He finally meets older men, the established swans, and he offers them his neck. They don't kill him, as maybe younger men would, they recognize him, and finally he is amongst his own.

His swan-ness represents his soul's purpose, the reason he was born. He starts off as a swan, he knows who he is and he is loved for it. Then through bitter experience he is led to believe he is something else, an Ugly Duckling. This is a hollow label and he struggles through much adversity to finally recognize himself. This represents our life's purpose - not our job, not our role as parent- but the being we really ought to be. It is very personal, and we recognize it when we feel happy, when we are at one with ourselves. We are in it when we are pursuing what we need to pursue, when we are doing what we were born to do. At that moment time stops, we are not conscious of other people, we are content, we are at peace, we are at one with nature. We don't need the company of others. That is how we recognize it, how we can come to identify ourselves, and what we should be doing with our lives. It is how we need to define our lives, not by how we please other people, but how we find pleasure within ourselves. Without loving ourselves we will never love others. It is a place of self-confidence.

How can we use this?

I find it difficult to suggest anything. Mainly because this is so far removed from our present day experience, it feels alien. Here we have a fully-grown mature man behaving as he should. Coming through danger and adversity, not being led by his ego, but having humility and grace. He has become an elder in the true sense of the word.

The only thing I can suggest is to grieve, cry real tears....
Feel how moving this passage is, and cry about it
Let the tears well up in your eyes and let them fall without reserve
Cry for his transformation
Cry for his despair in the moment of surrender
Cry for all the men who haven't done this work
Cry for all the boys who don't have these kinds of role models
Cry for all the women who don't know this is what they need
Cry for all our older people who didn't do this work
Cry for all our ancestors who forgot about it
Cry for all the indigenous peoples from every country of the world who were sacrificed at the altar
of progress and 'civilization', and are now disconnected to this way of being
Cry for the future generations that they might rediscover this way of being

152

Grief is a very beautiful cleansing process, men are as good at it as women, it is something to be proud of, not ashamed. The concept of 'machismo' has created a huge amount of damage in the world. Men do not loose their maleness by crying or by showing vulnerability. They actually honour their maturity and multi-layeredness by grieving, please remember this.

I know I have swallowed my grief on many occasions when I should have let it out, and I know by continually doing so I will create illness in my body. Grief doesn't have to be rational - it is just personal. The day my children left home was full of grief, but I bravely/stupidly showed none. The grief I feel on a regular basis in terms of the fact my children have left home and I don't see them from day to day, is immense. Some days it will overwhelm me from nowhere, and I just have to cry. I don't want my children to be with me every day, I know I can't turn back time, but there still remains a deep seated grief within me, and I now know this is natural, it is normal to feel this way. If you don't feel this way you have really cut yourself off from your emotions very severely. I was once told of a warrior people who judged their warriors by their ability to grieve each day, if they could cry every day then they were perceived to be good warriors. Those are my kind of people. The elders I want to work with will know what it means to grieve, and be proud of their ability to feel anguish and pain, they will be humble.

CHAPTER TWENTY-SIX
HUMILITY

The Story

Some children came out into the garden. They had brought bread with them to feed the swans. The youngest child shouted, "Look, there's a new one!" All the children joyfully clapped their hands, and they ran to tell their parents.

Cake and bread were cast on the water for the swans. Everyone agreed that the new swan was the most beautiful of them all. The older swans bowed towards him.

He felt so shy that he hid his head beneath his wing. He was too happy, but not proud, for a kind heart can never be proud. He thought of the time when he had been mocked and persecuted. And now everyone said that he was the most beautiful of the most beautiful birds. And the lilac bushes stretched their branches right down to the water for him. The sun shone so warm and brightly. He ruffled his feathers and raised his slender neck, while out of the joy in his heart, he thought, "Such happiness I did not dream of when I was the ugly duckling."

Interpretation of this part of the story

Finally the Ugly Duckling has reached the tenth stage of his rite, the celebration. The children are the next generation from the Ugly Duckling, already he is in his new role as elder. He is a beautiful role model for these young people, just by being himself. He isn't showing off, he's not pushing himself forward, and he's being natural. The older swans now bow to him, he is honoured by his elders –honoured for passing through his rite of passage – he is loved unreservedly. The older swans are recognizing something, an undeniable truth, which again we lost somewhere along the way. The next generation should always surpass the previous. I realized quite early on that I am a role model for my children, I can teach them, I can guide them. However, they are also able to take my teachings to the next stage, to a level of understanding I didn't see, I wasn't prepared for. The teacher becomes the pupil, the pupil becomes the teacher.

Resonance for us now

He acknowledges his past, he remembers how he was mocked and persecuted. He realizes he has transcended this. He no longer needs to blame anyone. He just is who he is, and the bad times are an intrinsic part of him. In our present culture we quite rightly try to protect our young and vulnerable ones from hardships and harm. My protective nature is very strong when I think of my children, and yet I know I have to trust them. I have to trust the love my wife and I gave them as children, and continue to give them, will be sufficient. Indeed, this story tells us, it is those moments when our children despair and are being hurt which are defining and important. In a sense we all know this, but many of us have tried to insulate ourselves, and our loved ones.

I guess the message is *"Stop trying to hold everything together"*. Stop stirring the waters of your ponds with your feet, stop clenching your teeth and smiling. Show some faith, not only in your children, but also yourself and other people. Let's stop being fearful about life, and start to celebrate it instead.

Examples from near and far

Everyone honours the Ugly Duckling by having a feast, cake and bread is cast on the water. This is the graduation ceremony to recognize he is through and into the next stage of his life. It is a reason for celebration, and these kinds of celebrations need to be huge. They need to reflect the significance the community feels such a graduation deserves. At the conclusion of the circumcision ritual for the Samburu boys, there is a graduation ceremony. This lasts for at least two days, if not more, and for each participating boy two animals are killed, normally, these are a bull and a goat. This is a hugely generous gesture in a semi-nomadic culture completely reliant on their livestock. The feast starts early in the morning with the ritual killing of the animals, over two hundred are killed in two days. The butchering takes many hours, and then the food is distributed within the tribe in a very strict way. The elders are given particular cuts of meat, the right leg for instance, the women receive the livers, kidneys and intestines, different generations eat different cuts of the animals. The fat from the bulls' chest is used by the initiate to smear onto the body of his best friend, to seal a bond of friendship to last a lifetime. It is a massive event, full of singing, dancing, socializing and feasting, it enables the boys to see how important the rites of passage is to the whole of the community. Those boys will always remember these events for the rest of their lives.

How can we use this?

I spoke with some of the elders of the Samburu about the significance of their rite of passage, and wanted to know what they felt about it. For them it represented a lifeline back to their ancestry. It also dictated the structure of their whole society, the age set system by which each generation is named, is the way in which they know who they are. I asked about the principles behind the ritual, and these are some of their thoughts, in no particular order. The programme is the rites of passage ritual which lasts up to 6 months, and which is undertaken every 15 years.

You are volunteered for the programme
The elders make all the decisions about who can participate and not
The elders must have undergone the programme themselves
The initiates must be taught, tested and challenged
The initiate must want to participate
The programme must be long and arduous otherwise the initiates won't bond
It must be hard enough for the initiates to fear failure
The whole programme must be decided by the elders
The initiates' parents must see the importance of the ritual and support it, even though they are not directly involved
The initiates need to be physically challenged, both in terms of their endurance and their ability to go without sleep
Blood needs to be shed
The teaching of the elders must be useful to the initiates
Repetitive singing and chanting must be part of the ritual
The initiate must work towards a goal, something very difficult

Once that goal has been achieved there needs to be a very big community celebration

There needs to be a 'passing out' ceremony

The younger boys who haven't been initiated must see the programme and want to be part of it

The graduates' relationship to his mother must be radically different at the end of the programme

The programme is about lessening his dependence on 'womanly' things, and increasing his interest in 'manly' things

The initiate must be given an older man on whom he can rely, and who will support him, not his father

The programme is just the start of a long process, up to 15 year long, ending in marriage

The programme teaches the initiate how difficult, complex and full of responsibility being a parent will be

The programme aims to make him step towards self reliance, but it will be many years before he can become it

The initiates learn about each other, their strengths and weaknesses

The initiates are introduced to the principles of sharing, and this must be practiced after graduation

The initiate must learn how to make fire

The initiates must despair

The initiates must be cocky

The initiates must feel exhausted

At the conclusion of the circumcision ritual and the graduation ceremony, the elders and I sat facing Mount Kenya to offer our thanks to N'gai (spirit). Within those prayers we thanked all those who had helped us and guided us through difficult times. One elder offered thanks to N'gai for allowing all the boys to live through the ritual. For the Samburu it was quite remarkable none of the boys had died, although one had come within ten minutes of loosing his life according to the doctors who saved him from bleeding to death after circumcision. The boys had undertaken arduous and dangerous treks into the wilderness; they had been force marched huge distances without food and water; they had cut and burnt themselves in preparation for the pain; and they had been humbled by the public circumcision in a remembrance of ancestral duty and responsibility. I witnessed probably the last time such a ritual will have been undertaken, and the bravery of those boys will stay with me forever. I do not suggest we should try to recreate such a brutal and dangerous ritual here in our civilized world. But, the principles and long-term consequence of such ritual is very much needed right now. To copy such an ancient and foreign ceremony would be absurd, but to ignore the need for such rites would also be negating our responsibility to the future generations.

How we create the next steps and stages will be vital for our survival on this planet, I am absolutely convinced of that. So, I look forward with anticipation and great expectation to the next twenty years of creativity, collaboration and humble adventures. May all men know they have a role and responsibility to the planet, and may they work in peace and harmony to co-create a future full of compassion, empathy and love in collaboration with the women of this world.

May we also learn how to celebrate, how to give thanks correctly. Rightly, we have dealt with grief in this book as it is a vital component in any rites of passage. However, grief is not a permanent state, and if it dealt with correctly it will naturally give way to joy. Unreserved, unconditional, expressions of community celebration are rare but extremely beautiful things. May we all be able to find our way back to such expressions, and may we share them with our children.

So many people bemoan the loss of community as being one of the major reasons for our present problems. As a community artist I was employed all over the world to create artifacts of beauty with large groups of people. They told the people's stories, and gave them an opportunity to express themselves. A hugely important part of the process was the celebration of completion. Everyone involved, their families, their friends, came together and gave praise. Such events create community. It can be a community lasting for one day, or a lifetime. I can't judge or know, all I can say is, those individuals will remember them for a long time. Part of building community is the mutual support inherent in celebration. I know it is vital, and that creativity and celebration are the glue binding a community together. We need to remember and re-create this.

In the Christian-Western tradition Christmas, New Year, and Easter are all we have left in terms of celebrations of our past, a dim memory of ceremony, and the coming together as a community. They are now commercial farces, they have sold their souls. We have prostituted our community celebrations to commercialism and the television. Those celebrations weren't genuine in the first place, the Christians stole and adapted them from the Pagans, who stole and adapted them from their ancestors. Let's forget about religion. Let's celebrate the fact we all live here and now, without having to buy a card, without having to spend money on it. If we can remember who we are, where we live, and reconnect to this land, our seasons, the beauty of our indigenous place, we might just be able to start to create new rituals and community celebrations that are valid, which have meaning. Meaning in terms of transcending religious barriers, identity barriers, colour barriers – celebrations transcending materialism. Community is created by ritual, by ceremony, we can't buy community, it is not for sale.

CONCLUSIONS

A One-Year Rite of Passage

The Ugly Duckling has been on a hugely challenging journey, and, for me, in this time he has developed into a whole human being. If I take the story very literally it has taken from his birth in the summer through to the spring for this transformation to happen. In terms of a teenager this could represent a yearlong rites of passage programme, which involved ten stages.

The first stage was to ascend
- he needed to fly away from his home at a high velocity fuelled by emotion.
The second stage was peer acceptance and initiation
— he found similar aged young men, they accepted him and invited him on an adventure.
The third stage was the wounding
— he came very close to death, and this shocked him.
The fourth stage was caution
— a natural reaction to the previous stage — but allied to being alone, rejecting previously help beliefs, the shedding of skins, the questioning of reality.
The fifth stage was the finding of his purpose
— making choices, starting to know what he wanted from life, starting to form his personality, the creation of his new identity as a man not a child.
The sixth stage was embarking on a vision quest
— seeking the future, trying to find signs confirming his new identity.
The seventh stage was descent
— a descent into facing his own darkness, slowing down, and starting to accept his fate.
The eighth stage was asking for help
— being found by an elder, being helped, and breaking down the ego.
The ninth stage was closure
— accepting his past, forgiving himself and everything.
The tenth stage was celebration
— a feast and recognition as he is accepted back into society.

I have used the Ugly Duckling to tell this tale and, of course, the story is inadequate. Hans Christian Andersen didn't write it as an allegory for rites of passage, he just wrote it. He is a single parent child and, in that sense, he illustrates the negative aspects of our present society very well. He undertakes his rite of passage alone, outside our society, and this is how we are presently forcing our teenagers to behave.

If he had elders to hold his passage then it would have been different. The first three stages would be the same. We cannot avoid our children making mistakes, indeed they need to do this. However, the fourth stage would have been him being given a

mentor or role model. The elder who took on this role could have:-
- *taught him about the natural world and his role within it*
- *set the young man to work with his hands*

For me these two elements are crucial in assisting young men to gain knowledge about themselves and the world. They represent the concept of apprenticeships and illustrate the way in which men teach - by example, not by talking or explaining. Understanding the natural world will give him a grounding and appreciation of the simple things in life. Working with his hands enables him to vacate his head or mind and be absorbed by other parts of himself. The loss and disconnection to these aspects of every day life is crippling our young people. They need to be competent in these two fields, they need to be able to identify nature and be able to work with wood, or a similar art or craft. In order to learn about these the boy needs a teacher, an elder.

If he then undertook a community held rite with a mentor he would experience all the other levels of rite, secure in the knowledge there was someone near him who had been through it themselves, and who could offer guidance and assistance. He would also undertake the rite as a group experience, not on his own. By doing this he will bond with his peers and form deep, meaningful friendships lasting a lifetime. The integration of rites of passage into the very fabric of a society creates community. For the Samburu the boy's rites of passage creates the name of the age set, it creates the identity of every generation, and without it they would literally be lost. With it, every Samburu can identify who you are, where you have been, and be safe around you. It defines the Samburu people, and we need to start to see quite what we have lost when we expect our teenagers to do this work by themselves. These are just the bare bones in terms of a rite of passage for a teenage lasting a year, they need to be complex and multi-layered.

If we are to start to re-introduce the ideal of community held rites of passage for teenagers there are so many things needing to be in place, which right now, are just not there. We would need competent elders, willing to commit themselves, able to commit themselves for such lengths of time. We would need teenagers who respected and wanted such a rite. We would need parents who would support it. We would need to work out how the rite would be structured and what it would contain in terms of challenge, threat, danger, reward and experience. We would need to know it would be valued, and even on completion of the tenth stage there would be further work to be undertaken, this is not a quick fix, and there may well be more mistakes and adventures along the way. A lot of work, but, I think, essential and vital work for our future generations.

By telling the story I have also touched on a great deal more than just the transition of a teenager. The Ugly Duckling relates to everyone, and we are all involved in these kinds of transformative processes. The journey is to make it intact from being a teenager through to becoming an elder. He illustrates vividly the transition from teenager into elder, which for me, is from about the age of 14 through to around 56. In this time you can make mistakes, have children, be bullied, work in the wrong jobs, loose hope, and experience despair. However, there is always the possibility you will come through this process and eventually forgive yourself and others, to become an elder. The story relates to a man and, being a man, I relate very much to the story. I believe elements of it can also apply to women, so I hope you will tolerate all the generalized statements made during the course of this book.

I am saddened to come to the end of the story and this book. I have enjoyed the exploration, and I hope it has been of value to you as well. I am happy to have explored The Ugly Duckling in relationship to rites of passage, but also issues around parenting and maleness, I know it has been very helpful for me. In conclusion, all I can say is this, please think about some of the issues in this book, and please do something about them if they strike a cord.

Extend the family

Hans Christian Andersen used his stories to write about his own life. He was a classic single-parent boy brought up by his mother, without a father. In today's society this is an increasingly common experience. We can all be critical of single parents and how they provide a limited experience for their children, but that is far too simplistic a view. I know all single parents desperately want to provide more for their children, they try their best, and who am I to judge. In our society we have created an ideal, a child with two parents. When there is a father and a mother for the child we somehow think this is complete. It is not. Even those children who have two parents are really struggling and their lives can be intolerably empty, without hope. Children need more than just a mother and a father, they need grandparents, uncles and aunts, they need an extended family participating directly in their upbringing, not one living hundreds of miles away, seen once a year. The extended family is the best way of bringing up a child, I have no doubt about this. It doesn't mean we are failing our children by not providing such. This is the ideal and we need to work towards it. I know a lot of people will disagree with me, but in a way, the increase in divorce and separation is leading to more extended families, and can in many cases be seen as beneficial to the child.

However, even an extended family is not enough, we should also have a wide range of role models, both male and female, for our children at different times in their lives. People who are not related but take an interest, members of our community. As the child becomes a teenager they need different types of influences to those they had as a child. They are spreading their wings, they go beyond the home and comfort of their familiar territories. The father and mother can't do the work, and often the extended family members are unwilling to involve themselves. You need to have a certain quality to be at ease with teenagers.

I guess what I'm coming to is the concept of Godparents, (an awful name) for teenagers. Adults who care for the children but who aren't necessarily connected by blood to them. Adults who have committed themselves to some form of care and re- sponsibility for the child and take the responsibility seriously. For me this, together with parents, together with grandparents, together with aunts and uncles, is the bare minimum in terms of support our children need in order to grown into sensible and whole human beings. A society providing these things for their young people would not have the social problems we face right now.

The future

I've enjoyed the opportunity the creation of this book has afforded. I have been given the chance to express myself. In so doing I have been able to talk about my past, my experiences, and my personal views. As I said at the beginning of the book, please don't think I'm trying to convert you to my way of thinking. I feel this book is just the start of a dialogue, needing many voices and many years to develop. I have worked with communities since 1975 - the problems then are the problems now. I believe rites of passage can bring about a profound change, if undertaken in the right way, they offer us hope in these dark times. In the early days of my work I would often be employed for a few hours to '*do art with children*', in many senses, it was just child minding. I know I can now offer something deeper, more profound, but it will take longer than a few hours. I am not alone in knowing this, and many of the people I meet who work with families, parents and communities feel the same way. They are anxious to step up to the next level of experience for their clients. To do so, will take courage, we may be mocked by others, and make mistakes, or experience failure. Personally, I have already started to do this work, so, please, join me in exploring the next stages of building community. There is no way back for me, being employed as a token artist will not suffice, I expect more from myself and from others. I thank Hans Christian Andersen for being part of that transitional journey for me. What a wonderful story '*The Ugly Duckling*' is. It has helped me through some very dark times. I hope it can help you to find what you need.

Whilst I was with the Samburu tribe in Kenya we had many heated discussions in terms of rites of passage, circumcision, and parenting in general. I have a great deal of respect for those people, but I was acutely aware their life style was coming to an end, they are no longer nomadic due to pressure of population, and many other factors. It is impossible for them to return to how things were one hundred years ago, our lifestyle and culture is starting to influence their everyday lives. With this change they are going to have to completely re-think their culture, and adopt some of our ways. A great deal of this will be for the better – the stopping of female circumcision, the education and employment of women, the non-acceptance of domestic violence – these are all positive influences. The reliance on money and material goods is however going to have a huge and damaging effect. The elders also knew the circumcision ritual for the boys will have to change, indeed it is less severe already, but they will fight desperately to retain the age set concept, and so they should. We discussed many different ideas and thoughts about how best to go about this transition. They already work collectively and mutually support each other, the land is owned communally, and they are setting up honey co-operatives, trying to be self reliant. As an outsider who was familiar with materialism and capitalism I was able to give them support and help which was appreciated. Trying to balance what they loose with what they will gain. In return they taught me a huge amount.

Then we took time to reflect on my own circumstances, and through discussion we realized my culture is at the same crossroads. We, in the West, can't turn back the clock, major change is just as inevitable in our lives as for the Samburu. The Samburu are looking to us for answers, and we in turn need to look to them for answers as well. The positive aspects of their lives, the extended family, the sharing of resources without ownership, the concepts of community belonging and individual responsibility all need to be revisited by us. In many ways we may look at the primitive people of the world and feel superior, knowing we have centrally heated homes, fast cars, and holidays in the sun. This is to miss the point. Inevitably these people will come into contact with our world and may well be impressed and enamored of it. We need to help them to adjust without selling their souls completely! We need to also change our lives for the better, whatever that may be. How we do any of this is up for grabs and will mean huge changes, just as much as the Samburu will have adapt and change. I look forward to the challenge and hope we can all bring about changes encouraging love, promoting equality and counteracting violence and war.

THE JOURNEY

I've tried to keep this book as simple as possible, thank you for coming with me on this journey and I appreciate your patience. I started writing in 2004, I never imagined how it would turn out. A lot of the content has come through me, I am shocked by some of the things I have written. Where did they come from? I don't know....an innate part of me, ignored and forgotten for some time. I have had to burn a huge amount of candles. I have made many offerings and sacrifices to the unknown in return for the privilege of being this channel.

I know I am a forgetful soul blundering around trying to find some vestiges of truth in my life and the wider world. I know I have gained so much from this process, I am not the man who started this journey, I have grown and come to some momentous decisions and conclusions in this time. I thank the spirits and guides who have pitied me during this short time and enabled me to pass on these messages.

Do with them as you wish. Blessings on their journey. I let them all go. I don't own them. This is just the start of the journey.

HANS CHRISTIAN ANDERSEN
(1805-1875)

Hans Christian Andersen was born in Odense, Denmark. We know quite a lot about him because almost all his books were autobiographical in nature. He used his storytelling skills as therapy. He was able to explore his own story through the development of these 'fairy tales'. His father was a shoemaker and he received little or no early education. When he was 11 his father died and he had to earn money for all the family. He was apprenticed to a weaver and a tailor, he also worked at a tobacco factory, but it seems he was not very good at being the breadwinner.

In 1819, at the age of 14, he moved to Copenhagen in an attempt to start a theatrical career, although he didn't really know what he wanted to do. He struggled hugely during this time, but eventually became associated with the Royal Theatre. At the age of 17, he had the opportunity to actually have an education for the first time and he went to the grammar school at Slagelse. Given that he was very tall for his age, and he was in a class full of 11 year olds, the ugly duckling story seems very relevant to this passage in his life. In 1828 he gained admission to Copenhagen University, where he completed his education.

In 1831 the first of his many travel sketches was published. As a novelist Andersen made his breakthrough with The Improvisatore (1835). Andersen's fame comes from his Fairy Tales and Stories, written between 1835 and 1872. The way in which he constructed his tales was unique at that time. He wrote them in a very modern way, in the style of spoken language rather than in a flowery or elaborate way.

For further reading about Hans Christian Andersen

Hans Christian Andersen by Rumer Godden (1955)
Hans Christian Andersen: The Story of His Life and Work 1805-75 by Elias Brendsdorff (1975)
H.C. Andersen by Erling Nielsen (1983)
The Kiss of the Snow Queen: Hans Christian Andersen and Man's Redemption by Woman by Wolfgang Lederer (1986)
The Amazing Paper Cuttings of Hans Christian Andersen by Beth Wagner Brust (1994)
Hans Christian Andersen: Danish Writer And Citizen Of The World by Sven Hakon Rossel (1996)
Hans Christian Andersen: The Life of a Storyteller by Jackie Wullschlager (2001)
Hans Christian Andersen: A Biography by R. Nisbet Bain (2002)

REFERENCES

1   Kenneth Meadows *"The Medicine Way"* (Dorset: Element 1990)
2   Jean Liedloff *"The Continuum Concept"* (London:Penguin 1989)
3   Steve Biddulph *"Manhood"* (Gloucestershire: Hawthorn Press 2002)
4   Robert Bly *"Iron John - A book about men"* (Dorset: Element 1990)
5   Malidoma Somé *"Ritual, Power, Healing and Community"* (Bath: Gateway Books, 2000)
6   Leonard Peltier *"Prison Writings – my life is my sundance"* (New York: St. Martin's Press, 1999)
7   Joseph Campbell *"The Hero With a Thousand Faces"* (Princetown: Princeton University Press, 1970)
8   Steven Foster and Meredith Little *"The Roaring of the Sacred River"* (California: Lost Borders, 1997)
9   Anthony De Mello *"Awareness"* (London: Fount 1990)
10   Dr. Mihaly Csikszentmihalyi *"Play and Intrinsic Reward"* Journal of Human Psychology 15, 3 (1975)
11   Thomas Moore *"Dark Nights of the Soul"* (London:Piatkus, 2004)
12   Steven Foster and Meredith Little *"The Roaring of the Sacred River"* (California: Lost Borders, 1997)
13   Shakti Gawain *"Return to the Garden"* (New York: Nataraj 1989)
14   Dr. M C Phillip and Stephanie Carr-Gomm *"The Druid Animal Oracle"* (Kent: Grange 2001)
15   Thomas Moore *"Dark Nights of the Soul"* (London:Piatkus, 2004)
16   Edmond Szekley, ed. and trans., *"The Gospel of Peace of Jesus Christ by the Disciple John"* (Berkeley: Shambala Press, 1970)
17   Thomas Moore *"Dark Nights of the Soul"* (London:Piatkus, 2004)
18   Ram Dass *"Still Here"* (New York: Penguin Putnam, 2000)
19   Kahil Gibran *"The Prophet"* (London: Heinemann, 1926)
20   Robert Bly *"Iron John - A book about men"* (Dorset: Element 1990)
21   Malidoma Somé *"Ritual, Power, Healing and Community"* (Bath: Gateway Books, 2000)

SELECTED BIBLIOGRAPHY

Antero Alli *"All Rites Reversed: Ritual technology for self-initiation"* (California:Vigilantero 1986)

Steve Biddulph *"Manhood"* (Sydney: Hawthorn Press 2002)

Robert Bly *"Iron John - A book about men"* (Dorset: Element 1990)

Pauline Campanelli *"Rites of Passage: The pagan wheel of life"* (Woodbury:Llewellyn, 1994)

Joseph Campbell *"The Hero With a Thousand Faces"* (Princetown: Princeton University Press, 1970)

Mark Carnes *"Secret Ritual & Manhood in Victorian America"* (Yale:Yale University, 1989)

Dr. Mihaly Csikszentmihalyi *"Play and Intrinsic Reward"* Journal of Human Psychology 15, 3 (1975)

Dr. Mihaly Csikszentmihalyi *"Flow:The Psychology of Optimal Experience"* First Edition (New York: Harper and Row, 1990)

Ram Dass *"Still Here"* (New York: Penguin Putnam, 2000)

David Dean *"Ravennetus"* (London: Pandea 1995)

Mircea Eliade *"Rites & Sumbols of Initiation:The mysteries of birth and rebirth"* (London :Harper, 1958)

A. P. Elkin *"The Australian Aborigine"* (Sydney:Angus and Robertson, 1943)

A. P. Elkin *"Aboriginal Men of High Degree: Initiation & sorcery in the world's oldest tradition"* (Sydney: Inner Traditions, 1994)

Alan Ereira *"The Heart of the World"* (London: Johnathan Cape, 1990)

Steven Foster and Meredith Little *"The Roaring of the Sacred River"* (California: Lost Borders, 1997)

H. W. Fowler and F.G. Fowler, ed. *"The Concise Oxford Dictionary"* (Oxford: Clarendon Press, 1964)

Betty Friedan *"The Feminist Mystique "* (New York; Norton 1963)

Shakti Gawain *"Return to the Garden"* (New York: Nataraj 1989)

Arnold Van Gennep *"Rites of Passage:A classic study of cultural celebrations"* (Chicargo: University of Chicago, 1960)

Kahil Gibran *"The Prophet"* (London: Heinemann, 1926)

James Hillman *"A Blue Fire"* (London: Harper Collins 1989)

Washington Irving *"The Rocky Mountains"* (Philadelphia: Carey, Lea, & Blanchard, 1837)

Tony Ivens and Nick Clements *"An Introduction to Working With Fathers"* (Wales: Fatherskills, 2005)

C. G. Jung *"Psyche and Symbol"* (Garden City, New York: Doubleday, 1958)

Tripora Klein *"Celebrating Life: Rites of passage for all ages"* (London:Delphi, 1992)

Maria Leach, ed. *"Standard Dictionary of Folklore, Mythology and Legend"* (San Fransisco: Harper and Row, 1972)

Thomas Leemon *"Rites of Passage in a Student Culture"* (Teachers College, 1972)

Jean Liedloff *"The Continuum Concept"* (London:Penguin 1989)

Louise Caarus Mahdi *"Betwixt & Between: Patterns of masculine and feminine initiation"* (Open Court, 1987)

Michael Meade *"Men & the Water of Life: Initiation & the tempering of men"* (London : Harper, 1993)

Kenneth Meadows `*The Medicine Way"* (Dorset: Element 1990)

Anthony De Mello *"Awareness"* (London: Fount) 1990

Alice Miller *"For Your Own Good"* (New York: Farrar, Straus and Giroux, 1983)

Alexander Mitscherlich *"Society Without the Father"* (London:Tavistock, 1969)

Thomas Moore *"Dark Nights of the Soul"* (London:Piatkus, 2004)

A.S. Neil *"Summerhill School: A new view of childhood"* (London: Penguin 1992)

Simon Ottenberg *"Boyhood Rituals in an African Society: An interpretation"* (University of Washington, 1989)

Leonard Peltier *"Prison Writings – my life is my sundance"* (New York: St. Martin's Press 1999)

Dr. M C Phillip and Stephanie Carr-Gomm *"The Druid Animal Oracle"* (Kent: Grange 2001)

Erin Pizzey *"Prone To Violence"* (London: Commoners 2006)

M. Scott Peck *"The Road Less Traveled: A New Psychology of Love, traditional Values and Spiritual Growth"* (New York: Simon & Schuster, 1978)

Martin Prechtel *"The Disobedience of the Daughter of the Sun"* (Cambridge.MA:Yellow Moon Press 2001)

Ray Raphael *"Men from the Boys: Rites of Passage in Male America"* (Univeristy of Ne-braska, 1988)

Carl Rogers *"The Quiet Revolutionary: An Oral History"* (New York: Penmarin, 2002)

Malidoma Some *"Of Water & the Spirit: Ritual, magic & initiation in the life of an African shaman"* (London:Tarcher/Putnam, 1994)

Malidoma Some *"The Healing Wisdom of Africa: Finding life purpose through nature, ritual and community"* (London:Tarcher/Putnam 1999)

Malidoma Somé *"Ritual, Power, Healing and Community"* (Bath: Gateway Books, 2000)

Hyemeyohsts Storm *"Seven Arrows"* (New York: Harper and Row, 1972)

Edmond Szekley, ed. and trans. *"The Gospel of Peace of Jesus Christ by the Disciple John"* (Berkeley: Shambala Press, 1970)

Kathleen Wall *"Lights of Passage: Rituals & rites of passage for the problems & pleasures of modern life"* (London:Harper, 1994)

Bernard Weiner *"Boy into Man: A fathers' guide to initiation of teenage sons"* (London: Transformation Press, 1992)

Other titles by the author include:-

MURALS, MOSAICS, MADNESS AND MYTHS
by Nick Clements

This full colour book documents the remarkable story of the 23 year odyssey, between 1981 and 2004, undertaken by The Pioneers, a group of community artists based in Cardiff. From their origins as a loose group of friends who ran a gallery, they developed into professional community artists working all over the world. The story is unique in the history of British arts, it is one of incredible determination, imagination and inspiration.

The book includes a wide range of projects, documented through their stories and photographs. It is a frank account full of humour and excitement. It will encourage creative people to work collaboratively, and to stretch their creativity into new and exciting areas.

Published by
Sound of the Heart
ISBN 0-9547302-0-8

CREATIVE COLLABORATION
by Nick Clements

This book deals with the historical context of community art, how it has developed and the potential that it holds. Looking from a personal point of view at the importance of creativity and collaboration in the evolution of mankind as a species, and the ways in which we have used creativity and collaboration to create civilisation. The publication develops ideas about the importance of the work of artists and craftspeople in history and the way in which their significance has been eroded and forgotten.

A radical and extraordinary book which challenges the present art dogmas and beliefs. It offers new and innovative approaches to create remarkable new ways of living, collaborating and developing society. It offers inspiration and guidance to those who want to create such opportunities in the future.

Published by
Sound of the Heart
ISBN 0-9547302-1-6

PIONEERS IMPROVING YOUR SCHOOL ENVIRONMENT
by Nick Clements and Sarah Osborne

This book will inspire parents and teachers to think about ways of improving the educational experience of the children in schools. The expertise which The Pioneers gained applied to nursery, primary and secondary schools. This publication explains in simple stages how you can plan and develop your improvement strategy and it is illustrated by examples of work made by schools in South Wales, an area well known for its community spirit, but severely lacking in financial support systems. Yet despite these restrictions The Pioneers worked with over 35,000 children and raised in excess of £5 million towards the work.

Illustrated in full colour throughout with simple descriptions of how to design, create and make a wide range of visual art and craft projects in schools and other community settings.

Published by
NSEAD
ISBN 0-904684-17-2

AN INTRODUCTION TO WORKING WITH FATHERS
by Tony Ivens and Nick Clements

A book suitable for professionals working with fathers and father figures. Written by two fathers who have a great deal of experience and knowledge, not only from bringing up their own children, but also working in this field for over 30 years.

This is a unique and informative guide to working with fathers. Giving details and training ideas in terms of recruiting, developing and understanding how to undertake this important work. The book accompanies the training programme of the same name run by Fatherskills

Published by
Fatherskills
ISBN: 0-9551725-0-0

The next book in this series:

THE SEVEN AGES OF MEN
by Nick Clements

This book offers a new way of understanding maleness, and is a guide to the maturation process necessary for a boy to become a man, and how to create energetic and positive older men. It shows how all the recent changes in society, and the new ways in which humans relate to each other can be assimilated into a new maleness. The new man doesn't have to wear sandals and eat quiche, he can combine his sensitivity with his masculine enthusiasm and joy, he can evolve.

This book describes the series of ages and allied rites of passage which men need to undergo to reach 'eldership'. It clearly defines the qualities all men need to possess. It explains how the rites of passage allow each man to gain knowledge about the qualities he needs to be successful in the next age. It explains how lifestyle, life choices and quality of life can be dramatically improved when these structures are in place in our lives.

To Be Published by
Sound of the heart

All publications available from: www.soundoftheheart.com